Dinah Maria Mulock Craik

King Arthur

Not a Love Story

Dinah Maria Mulock Craik

King Arthur

Not a Love Story

ISBN/EAN: 9783743313873

Manufactured in Europe, USA, Canada, Australia, Japa

Cover: Foto ©ninafisch / pixelio.de

Manufactured and distributed by brebook publishing software (www.brebook.com)

Dinah Maria Mulock Craik

King Arthur

KING ARTHUR

Not a Love Story

BY THE AUTHOR OF
"JOHN HALIFAX, GENTLEMAN," &c.

NEW YORK
HARPER & BROTHERS, FRANKLIN SQUARE

MISS MULOCK'S WORKS.

ABOUT MONEY AND OTHER THINGS. 12mo, Cloth, 90 cents.
A BRAVE LADY. Illustrated. 12mo, Cloth, 90 cents.
A FRENCH COUNTRY FAMILY. Translated. Illustrated. 12mo, Cloth, $1.50.
AGATHA'S HUSBAND. 8vo, Paper, 35 cents; 12mo, Cloth, 90 cents.
A HERO, &c. 12mo, Cloth, 90 cents.
A LEGACY: The Life and Remains of John Martin. 12mo, Cloth, 90 cents.
A LIFE FOR A LIFE. 8vo, Paper, 40 cents; 12mo, Cloth, 90 cents.
A NOBLE LIFE. 12mo, Cloth, 90 cents.
AVILLION, &c. 8vo, Paper, 60 cents.
CHRISTIAN'S MISTAKE. 12mo, Cloth, 90 cents.
FAIR FRANCE. 12mo, Cloth, $1.50.
HANNAH. Illustrated. 8vo, Paper, 35 cents; 12mo, Cloth, 90 cents.
HIS LITTLE MOTHER, &c. 12mo, Cloth, 90 cents; 4to, Paper, 10 cents.
JOHN HALIFAX, GENTLEMAN. 8vo, Paper, 50 cents; 12mo, Cloth, 90 cents; 4to, Paper, 15 cents.
KING ARTHUR. 12mo, Cloth, 90 cents; Paper, 35 cents.
MISS TOMMY, and IN A HOUSE-BOAT. Illustrated. 12mo, Cloth, 90 cents; Paper, 50 cents.
MISTRESS AND MAID. 8vo, Paper, 30 cents; 12mo, Cloth, 90 cents.
MY MOTHER AND I. Illustrated. 8vo, Paper, 40 cents; 12mo, Cloth, 90 cents.
OLIVE. 8vo, Paper, 35 cents; 12mo, Cloth, Illustrated, 90 cents.
PLAIN-SPEAKING. 12mo, Cloth, 90 cents; 4to, Paper, 15 cents.
SERMONS OUT OF CHURCH. 12mo, Cloth, 90 cents.
THE HEAD OF THE FAMILY. 12mo, Cloth, Illustrated, 90 cents.
STUDIES FROM LIFE. 12mo, Cloth, 90 cents.
THE LAUREL BUSH. Illustrated. 12mo, Cloth, 90 cents.
THE OGILVIES. 8vo, Paper, 35 cents; 12mo, Cloth, Illustrated, 90 cents.
THE UNKIND WORD, &c. 12mo, Cloth, 90 cts.
THE WOMAN'S KINGDOM. Illustrated. 8vo, Paper, 60 cents; 12mo, Cloth, 90 cents.
TWO MARRIAGES. 12mo, Cloth, 90 cents.
YOUNG MRS. JARDINE. 12mo, Cloth, 90 cents; 4to, Paper, 10 cents.

BOOKS FOR CHILDREN.

FAIRY BOOK. 12mo, Cloth, 90 cents.
MOTHERLESS. Translated. Illustrated. For Girls in their Teens. 12mo, Cloth, $1.50.
SONGS OF OUR YOUTH. Poetry and Music. Square 4to, Cloth, $2.50.
THE ADVENTURES OF A BROWNIE. Illustrated. Square 16mo, Cloth, 90 cents.
THE LITTLE LAME PRINCE. Illustrated. Square 16mo, Cloth, $1.00.
OUR YEAR. Illustrated. 16mo, Cloth, $1.00.

GIRLS' BOOKS, Written or Edited by the Author of "John Halifax:"
LITTLE SUNSHINE'S HOLIDAY. 16mo, Cloth, 90 cents.
THE COUSIN FROM INDIA. 16mo, Cloth, 90 cents.
TWENTY YEARS AGO. 16mo, Cloth, 90 cents.
IS IT TRUE? 16mo, Cloth, 90 cents.
AN ONLY SISTER. 16mo, Cloth, 90 cts.
MISS MOORE. 16mo, Cloth, 90 cents.

PUBLISHED BY HARPER & BROTHERS, NEW YORK.

☞ *Sent by mail, postage prepaid, to any part of the United States or Canada, on receipt of price.*

PREFACE.

This book is founded on facts, which happened a good many years ago in America; the adopting parents were American; the child died young. I have re-told the story, with necessary artistic variations, because it teaches truths not always recognized. The world, voluble enough on the duties of children to parents, is strangely silent on the far more momentous ones of parents to children. This simple, and in the main point true tale, may suggest to some thoughtless readers what the Heavenly Father means when He sends to earthly fathers and mothers the blessing, and responsibility of a child.

Digitized by the Internet Archive
in 2007 with funding from
Microsoft Corporation

http://www.archive.org/details/kingarthurnotlov00crairich

KING ARTHUR.

NOT A LOVE STORY.

CHAPTER I.

FULLY twenty years before the great St. Gothard tunnel was made or thought of, when Andermatt was still the favorite resting-place of travelers passing from Switzerland into Italy, and *vice versâ*, a group of half a dozen persons sat round the *table d'hôte* of the principal hotel there, eating their rather meagre dinner. For it was early in June, and the stream of regular tourists had not yet begun to flow.

Not at any season do travelers pause long here, the valley of Uri being considered by pleasure-seekers in general a rather dull place. Perhaps; and yet it has its charms. It is a high level plateau, solemn and still, in the heart of the Alps. Through it comes pouring down the wild river Reuss, and up from it climb three desolate mountain roads, leading to three well-known passes—the St. Gothard, the Furca, and the Oberalp.

The valley itself is smooth and green, though too high above the level of the sea to be very fertile. Little corn is grown there, and the trees are few and small, but the pasturage during the brief summer—only three months—is abundant, and extending far up the mountain sides. Every yard of available land is cultivated, and the ground is "*parsemé*" (to use a French word for which there is no English equivalent), with that mass of wild flowers which makes Switzerland in June a perfect garden wherever you turn your eyes.

But these and all other beauties of the place were invisible to the travelers, for a dense white mist had suddenly come down and blotted out everything.

"To-day would have been worse even than yesterday for those young fellows to have crossed the St. Gothard from Italy, as they told me they did," said one of the three quiet English-speaking guests at the head of the table, looking across at the three voluble Italians at the foot of it.

"Scarcely more detestable weather than when we crossed, doctor. My wife has taken all these five days to get over it; and is hardly well yet."

"Oh yes, dear," said the lady—the only lady at table —small and ordinary in appearance, but with a soft voice and sweet eyes, which continually sought her husband's. He was tall, thin, and serious: in fact, had taken the head of the table and said grace in unmistakable clerical fashion. He looked the very picture of an English clergyman, and she of a clergyman's wife. One seemed about forty, the other fifty years old.

The third traveler, addressed as "Doctor," was not English, though he spoke our language with a far better pronunciation than most of us do. But he spoke it with a slight nasal twang, said to be inevitable, in consequence of climate, with our Transatlantic cousins. Also he had a gaunt, lean, dried-up appearance; but his long bony limbs were agile and strong, and his brown face was both shrewd and kindly; full of humor, yet at the same time full of tenderness, with no small amount of capacity as well.

"My dear Mrs. Trevena, I guess we had the devil's own weather (begging your pardon!) that day we crossed from Italy. When the snows begin to melt the Pass is worse and more dangerous than in the middle of winter. And in addition, we had that soaking rain. I am sure I was drenched to the skin for eight mortal hours. Medically speaking, I wonder any one of us, especially the women, came through the journey alive. But you say you're all right now, ma'am?"

"Oh yes," answered Mrs. Trevena, smiling. She seemed a person so accustomed to be "not strong," that she preferred to smile at illness, and make as light of it as possible. "I only hope the other two women—the only women who were in the sledges besides myself—came off as easily. I suppose they went on at once, for I have not seen them in the hotel since. Have you, Dr. Franklin?"

"Yes," said the doctor. He was not a man of many words.

"Are they here still, do you know?"

"Yes," he answered again, with still greater abruptness and brevity.

"I wish I had known it, and I would have inquired how they were. I felt so sorry for the lady—she was certainly a lady, though she was shabbily dressed, and so muffled up, it was almost impossible to see her face.

The old mulatto woman, who seemed her maid, was very anxious over her. They had not half wraps enough—yet when I offered her a rug she refused it with a mere shake of the head. She couldn't be English, or, hearing me speak, she would surely have spoken."

"No—not English."

"What was she then? German?"

"American. My dear lady, you will not find two mouthfuls on that *poulet*. It looks more like an overgrown sparrow; really, the food here is abominable."

"No wonder," said the clergyman mildly. "I believe they have to carry up nearly everything from the valleys below—several thousand feet. Nothing will grow here—not even the chickens. What a place Andermatt must be to live at in winter!"

"Yet they do live here. Madame told me to-day—so far as I could understand her English—I wish I spoke better French, Austin!—that they keep the hotel open all winter. Her elder children go to school at Lucerne, but the two little boys learn from the *pasteur* here. They go to him every day in a sledge, drawn by Juno, the huge St. Bernard who is always lying at the hotel door."

"Listen to her!" said the grave clergyman, turning upon the little sweet-faced woman an affectionate look. "I do believe if my wife were dropped down in the wilds of Africa, within three days she would have made friends with all the blackamoors, big and little—especially the little ones—have found out all their affairs, and been made the confidante of all their sorrows."

"In the language of signs—as now," laughed Mrs. Trevena.

"Never mind, ma'am; you manage somehow. Madame's poor little boy with the broken leg and his German *bonne* look out for your daily visit with great excitement. I guess they'll miss you when you go away."

"And I shall miss Andermatt. I like the place; it is so quiet—so utterly out of the world. And the hotel-people are so simple and good; I seem to know all about everybody."

"Do you, ma'am?" said the doctor, with a sharp questioning look, which fell harmless on the innocent face; then, apparently satisfied, he added, "How valuable your wife must be in your parish at home, Mr. Trevena!"

"Invaluable—except that it is so small a parish. But we hope for a better living by and by. We have been hoping all our lives," added he, with a slight sigh.

"But we do sometimes get what we hope for, Austin," said his wife. "You cannot think, Dr. Franklin, how he has enjoyed his three months' chaplaincy at the Italian lakes—such a lovely spring! and we are going back to a second spring—or rather summer—in England. We live in the country—in Cornwall."

"A region which very likely Dr. Franklin never heard of; but we think a great deal of it, being both of us Cornish-born," said Mr. Trevena. He was a little slow in speech and formal in manner—this old-fashioned English gentleman; and the quick, keen, energetic American regarded him with the interest of a student of human nature, who had discovered a new phase thereof. They were very different; but both being rarely honest and good men, they had fallen into a sort of liking; and during the six days they had been weather-bound at Andermatt, had become tolerably intimate.

Their not too luxurious meal over, the three English-speaking inmates of the hotel still sat on at the *table d'hôte;* comparatively silent—at least when contrasted with the voluble young Italians below.

"What can they be talking about, so fast and furious—almost as if they were going to fight?" said Mrs. Trevena, somewhat amused, while her husband looked annoyed—as a Briton often does at anything foreign which he does not understand. But the more cosmopolite American only laughed. He had traveled through many lands on both sides the ocean; he spoke at least three Continental tongues, and had been a great help in that and other ways to the English parson, who knew no modern language but his own.

"Why cannot people converse without gesticulating like savages and looking as if they were about to tear one another to pieces," observed he, in some irritation.

"Not at all!" laughed the Kentuckian. "They are the best of friends. Two of them belong to the Teatro at Milan, sent in pursuit of a singer there, who has broken her engagement, and gone off, it is supposed, to London or Paris in search of a better one. They don't think her flight implies anything worse than love of money; they say the Signora had no lovers—only a husband, and perhaps a bad one."

"Poor lady!" said Mrs. Trevena. "But if she were a real lady she would never be an opera-singer. What a dreadful life it must be!"

The doctor laughed in his dry way—he was more of a

laughing than a weeping philosopher, and of practical rather than sentimental mind—then looked at his watch. "Excuse me; I have a visit to pay this evening."

"Is it to Madame's little boy with the broken leg? Then I will go first, just for a minute, and leave some pictures to amuse him—poor little patient soul!"

"That is just like my wife," said Mr. Trevena, looking after her with a smile that ended in a sigh.

"Mrs. Trevena seems uncommonly fond of children. Perhaps she has left some behind her at home? I'm a family-man myself; and after two years in Europe I shan't be sorry to see those ten little shavers of mine in Kentucky."

"Ten, have you? We have none. We had one—but it only lived a few hours. My wife has never quite got over the disappointment; and it was to give her a total change for mind and body that I accepted the chaplaincy abroad. We have only been married three years, though we waited for fifteen," added the good man with the faintest shade of a blush on his calm middle-aged face. "I was a Fellow of my College, and at last I got a College living—rather a poor one. But we are very happy—my wife and I. We shall at least end our days together."

"Phew!" said the American, repressing a low whistle, while his kindly eyes took a curiously soft expression as they rested on his companion. He had had a fairly happy life himself, and his "ten little shavers" were obviously very dear to him. "She's a good woman—your wife," continued he bluntly. "So is mine. I'd lay you a dollar against ten cents, you'll not find such a mother anywhere as Mrs. Franklin. I wish all women were like our two, sir."

"I hope many women are," answered the mild clergyman—adding anxiously, "Do not speak to Mrs. Trevena of what I told you—her lost child. It is a sore place in her heart still; never likely to be healed. But we have made up our minds to be content: and we are content. God knows best."

"I suppose so."

"I am sure so; and I am a much older man than you. Isn't it strange," continued the clergyman, laying his hand kindly on the doctor's arm, "that you and I should have talked of this and many other things—we who never met before, and in all probability shall never meet again?"

"Perhaps for that very reason; I have often found it so. People tell me things that they wouldn't tell their most intimate friends. You have no idea the odd secrets and odd people that I have come across during my life. By Jove—what a bother it is sometimes! But I beg your pardon—I was thinking of something else—something not too agreeable. And now I must go to my patient—who is not, as your wife imagined, the little broken-legged boy. However, in our profession we learn one good thing—to hold our tongues. Good-night, sir."

"Good-night, doctor. You'll drive up to Hospenthal with us, as my wife wishes, if it is a fine day to-morrow, and your patient can spare you?"

"Oh yes—yes. She——" Here Dr. Franklin set his lips together and clenched his fist, as if to beat himself for nearly letting a cat jump out of the bag. "Certainly—certainly! Good-evening."

He left the room by one door just as Mrs. Trevena entered by another. Her husband greeted her with a smile—the welcoming smile of those who have been necessary to one another for years, who never weary of each other's company, because it scarcely is company—the two having so grown together in all their tastes and habits that they feel like one. If the little life that had come, and then

>"Unto stillness passed again
>And left a blank, unknown before"—

had been a loss to them, it had undoubtedly but

>"Made them love the more."

That is, if more were possible. But the more or the less with regard to love is a question that chiefly troubles younger folk. The old accept it—only too thankfully—and cease to investigate it, or to weigh and measure it, any more than their daily sunshine or the air they breathe.

"The mist has lifted, Austin, and there is promise of a good sunset—as much as the mountains will let us see of it; and a full moon will soon be creeping over those white peaks opposite. Hark!—there are the bells of the cattle coming home. Are you ready for a walk, dear?"

"Quite ready, Susannah."

"Shall we go to the Devil's Bridge—or up towards Hospenthal? No, for we shall be driving that way to-morrow. I should like to get as far up as the Hospice, and be close under the eternal snows once again—see them in sunshine and calm, instead of such a deluge of rain as the day we crossed from Airolo."

"I wonder it did not give you your death of cold, my poor wife."

"Those other two women—the old and the young one—were worse off than I, for they had nobody to take care of them"—and she patted softly her husband's shoulder. "I felt so sorry for them. I have often thought of them since."

"You think of everybody, Susannah—except yourself. Come along! and as we go you can tell me what you think about one thing—our getting back as fast as we can to England."

"Very well, dear."

Somehow, though she was mild-faced, quiet, and small, and he was big and hale—even young-looking for his years—it was evident the good clergyman leant upon his wife not a little. And there was that in Mrs. Trevena's sweet composure which implied, not the perpetual acquiescence, feeble and flaccid, which some men think would be so delightful to have—until they get it; but an amount of dormant force, invaluable in the mistress of a household. She is no "perfect woman" who is not at the same time

"Nobly planned
To warn, to comfort, and command;"

and gentle as Mrs. Trevena looked, a keen observer could detect in her firm little mouth and quiet, silent ways, indications of strength and decision, which doubtless would prove the greatest possible blessing to the

Reverend Austin. Not that "the gray mare was the better horse!" for he looked—and was—the most excellent of men, and clergymen; but it was in many things the more useful horse, which fact often makes a pair run all the safer together. Austin Trevena, a student and a bookworm all his days, would have been practically "nowhere" in the busy world, but for his wife; who loved him perhaps all the dearer for his very weaknesses. His strength—which lay in his brains, and in a moral nature of such high chivalric honor that he would have gone to the stake without a murmur or a doubt—she more than loved—she worshiped. It had cost her some pangs, and a good many long lonely years, but she worshiped it still.

Enough, however, of these two, who had been such a deep interest to Dr. Franklin, in his capacity of student of human nature, that he had stayed on at Andermatt chiefly because they stayed. Also for another reason which with the reticence due his profession he did not name. When they met him going out, and asked him to accompany them in their evening saunter to the Devil's Bridge, he shook his head.

"I've got a Devil's Bridge of my own to cross—and I wish to heaven I knew how to manage it," said he. "Good-evening—I'll see you at breakfast to-morrow."

"And go with us up to the Hospice?"

"If I can. *Au revoir.*"

"He looks anxious and troubled about something," observed Mrs. Trevena, when the placid pair went on their way; stopping sometimes to watch the twilight colors on the mountains, and listen to the tinkle of the cattle-bells, as, one after the other, whole herds of the lovely little Swiss cows crept musically home.

"I suspect, my dear, that like another person I know, the good doctor often troubles himself with the troubles of other people. He told me he had a patient here—not your little sick boy—possibly some case of serious illness."

"I never heard of any, and I think I should have heard. Madame and I have grown to be very good friends."

"But Madame is a shrewd woman, who probably knows how to keep her own counsel, and not drive away her very few customers by rumors of sickness or death in the house."

"Death in the house? You don't think that, Austin? If I could be of any use——"

"You are of most use to me, Susannah, by not wearing yourself out over other folk; so don't put on that poor little anxious face, but let us enjoy our walk. We, thank heaven! have nobody but our two selves to be anxious over."

"No," answered his wife softly. But whether she thanked heaven—heaven only knew. It was one of those unconscious stabs which even the dearest sometimes give; and which heaven only can heal.

So they strolled on, sometimes talking, sometimes silent, in that happy companionship—just "one and one" —without need of a "shadowy third," which is the solace of many childless couples, and which, so long as it steers clear of that fatal dual selfishness which is the bane of conjugal life, is a most enviable and desirable thing.

They saw the sun set, the moon rise—at least by reflection, for the actual sunset and moonrise were of course invisible behind the mountains; and then they watched the stars come out like jewels in the great blue arch which seemed to rest on the high peaks of the St. Gothard range, white with eternal snow. When they returned, night had already fallen; a glimmering light up at Hospenthal, and another which burnt steadily on till morning in the Andermatt Hotel below, alone testified to the presence of any human existence in the silent valley.

Next day, at the *table d'hôte* breakfast, the English and American travelers alone remained; the Italians had vanished. Mr. and Mrs. Trevena looked placid and wholesome—as usual—in mind and body; but Dr. Franklin seemed tired and worried; or, as he expressed it, "seedy"; as if he had been up all night—which he owned he had.

"But why?" asked Mrs. Trevena, and then drew back and blushed for the intrusive question.

"Work, my dear lady—a doctor's work never ends. But now I mean to take a few hours' play. What time shall we start? We can drive up as far as the eternal snow, and down again, before dark."

"Easily."

"All right then. I'm your man. Off we go. I'll halve the carriage with you."

"Certainly not; we shall be glad of your company," said the English clergyman, with stately dignity, and despite his wife's rather pathetic look—which convinced the honest, warm-hearted American that "halving the

B

carriage" was a matter of importance to them, Mr. Trevena held to his point, and Dr. Franklin was obliged to yield.

They started. It was one of those gorgeous days—all blueness and whiteness, and flooded with dazzling, cloudless sunshine—which in Switzerland come as such a strange contrast to the days of mist and storm. The three friends, so lately strangers, found themselves ascending cheerily the mountain, past the tiny village of Hospenthal and the glacier of St. Anna; crossing the wild river Reuss, which came pouring down the desolate valley; and watching how the vegetation, at first bright as the colors of a kaleidoscope with masses of lovely unknown flowers, gradually dwindled—ceased; until the gray of the huge boulders, the intense blue of the sky, and the dazzling whiteness of the mountain slopes, were the only colors left. The road became steeper and steeper, and occasionally was fenced on either side by huge walls of unmelted, and apparently never-to-be-melted snow.

"You had better put on your blue veil, Mrs. Trevena, and here is a pair of blue spectacles for your husband—I wouldn't sacrifice my eyes for the grandest snow-landscape in the world. Nor my meals; but I see you have provided against mountain-hunger. Is that another fine, fat—sparrow?"

She laughed, as people do whose hearts are full, then said, with the tears in her eyes, "How beautiful all is! My whole life through I have longed to come here, and now I am here—we are here together, Austin. We should be very thankful."

"I think we are, Susannah," the clergyman said, in his grave, tender way. And then the two men—so very different outside, and yet with a certain sympathetic union at heart—sat down on either side the little woman, on what they called a "comfortable" stone, just below the shining wall of snow, forty feet high, which reflected the rays of the sun so as to be oppressively warm.

"Isn't it curious, Mrs. Trevena? though we sit under a wall of snow we are almost 'baked alive'—as my little monkeys in Kentucky would say." And stretching out his hand, he washed down the leg of chicken with a mouthful of snow, declaring it was "not bad drink after all."

"Does this huge white wall never melt?"

"Never entirely, ma'am" (his invariable "ma'am" and "sir," were so anti-English). "We are just on the verge of the snow-line—perpetual snow. And yet, just look at that patch of blue gentian—isn't it lovely? Are you a botanist, Mr. Trevena?"

"Oh no, but my wife is. At least, she has what I call a speaking acquaintance with almost every flower that grows. She knows their separate faces as well as those of the babies of our parish,—which seem to me all alike."

"Not a bit alike, when you are a woman and love them," said the wife, smiling.

"You seem very fond of children, Mrs. Trevena."

"Yes," she answered quietly—so quietly that the good doctor, feeling as if he could have bitten his tongue off for the remark, rose and proposed a saunter a little higher up the mountain.

"Decidedly. And my wife can rest here. She never

minds being left alone. I tell her it is because she finds her own company so pleasant, and no wonder!" added he, with affectionate courtesy.

"She's a trump," said the American—rough, candid, and kindly, as they walked away.

When they were out of sight and hearing of Mrs. Trevena, he suddenly stopped, and stuck his stick violently into a fast melting mass of snow.

"It's no use, sir, I can't stand it any longer; I must tell somebody."

"Tell what?" said the placid clergyman, very much surprised.

"Something which I have been expecting your wife would find out every day, but she has not done so. Madame has kept the secret well. I have often wished I could tell it to Mrs. Trevena, who has such capital common sense and right feeling—womanly feeling. Some women seem as if they had none at all; the fashionable life or the public life—Lord knows which, for I don't!—has taken all ordinary flesh and blood out of them. It does sometimes."

Mr. Trevena listened to this tirade with a perplexity which his politeness vainly tried to hide. "If there is anything you would like to confide in me—anything wherein I could be of use—according to my sacred profession."

"Mine has its sacredness too, if people only knew it. Many a troublesome secret have I kept; but this one—I can't keep it—I won't keep it; for, in a sense, it's like conniving at a murder. The massacre of the innocents I call it—and so I told the woman."

"What woman?" asked Mr. Trevena, now thoroughly aroused and uneasy—so uneasy, that he looked instinctively back at the little dark figure sitting motionless under the snow-wall, his wife, with whom he was accustomed to halve all his anxieties.

"No—don't tell her—not till we get back to the hotel. You may then; for, after all, she will understand it better than you, or than any man among us all."

And then he detailed how his mysterious patient, on whose account he had lingered these five days at Andermatt, was a lady—the lady with the mulatto servant who had crossed the St. Gothard the same day as themselves, and that very night had suddenly given birth to a child, with no help except the old woman, and no preparation for her infant except a few clothes borrowed from the kind landlady of the hotel—who, at the mother's urgent entreaty, had kept the event a secret from everybody.

"But she insisted on fetching me, as I spoke their language—both the black and the white woman are, I am sorry to say, American born. I told them in good plain English that they were both fools—or worse—to have attempted such a journey. It was a miracle that the mother and child survived—the child nearly was dead—and when I told her it lived, her first word was, that she was 'very sorry!' A mother indeed—a brute! No—any brute beast would have been more of a mother."

"Perhaps," suggested Mr. Trevena, with a faint old-bachelor-like blush—" perhaps she had some very strong reason for wishing it dead."

"Illegitimacy, you mean," interrupted the point-blank doctor. "No, I believe not. She had a wedding-ring on her finger, and in her delirium she talked of 'my goose of a husband' and 'my horrid little brats at home.' Therefore, I conclude she has both a home and a husband. Though why she should have gone wandering about the world in this insane manner is more than I can tell. Both she and her servant are absolutely silent."

"About how old is she?"

"Just under forty, I should say. Very handsome still—in a sort of way. Has had four children, but declares she 'hated every one of them the minute they were born.' Did you ever hear of such a woman?"

Mr. Trevena shook his head helplessly. "Well, my dear doctor, what can I do? Would you like me, in my clerical capacity, to pay her a visit?"

"Bless my life—no! She would laugh you to scorn —she laughs at everything serious, except when she gets into her tragedy-fits, when she rants for all the world like a play-actor—or actress."

"Perhaps she is an actress."

"May be—I never thought of that. But I have not thought much about her, except as a 'case,' till to-day. It was hard work to keep her alive at all—or the baby either—for she refused to suckle it. She said she wanted it to die; and if it had not been for a blessed old Nanny-goat of Madame's she'd have had her wish by this time. Now I think he'll do, for he is quite healthy; and such a fine, fat little fellow. Many a one of your childless English dukes—your 'noble families' that dwindle down to nothing and die out—would give his eyes for such a son and heir."

"A strange story," said Mr. Trevena thoughtfully. "May I tell my wife? She would be so much interested."

"Yes, and ask her to advise me: a woman—that is, a sensible woman—often leaps by instinct to the right, when a man with his long-headed wisdom goes swithering to and fro, till he finds himself quite at sea—as I own I am. That horrible creature! What do you think she asked of me last night?—To take away her child and leave it at the nearest Foundling Hospital—or by the roadside if I chose, for some charitable soul to pick it up! She doesn't care what becomes of it, so that she gets rid of it. She would sell it, she declares, for she wants money badly—only a baby is a drug in the market—a commodity no one cares to buy!"

"What a wretch!—oh dear, oh dear!" murmured the horrified and perplexed clergyman. "Surely she must be mad."

"Not at all; she is as sane as I am, a capable, clever, healthy woman. She must have a constitution of iron to have struggled through these few days; and she is doing very well now. She talks of continuing her journey immediately."

"Where to? Has she no friends?"

"None, she declares, except her 'fool of a husband,' whom she left six months ago, and has scarcely heard of since. She refuses to give her name or address. So—what can I do? She is my country-woman, and after all, a woman—or I would do nothing at all. She expects me to give her an answer to-night."

"About what?"

"About the Foundling Hospital. There are such in Switzerland, I know; but I can't present myself there with an unknown new-born baby in my arms—a decent father of a family like me. And if I leave the child with its mother, very likely she'll murder it, or neglect it till it dies—which is as bad as murder."

"But there is the mulatto woman; she may have a heart in her bosom if the mother has none."

"My dear sir, had you lived as long as I have in our Southern States, you would know that our niggers have big hearts, but mighty little heads, and no consciences to speak of. If that woman told her servant, who is a paid slave, to lie down and be walked upon, she'd do it; and if she bade her throw the child on the back of the fire, she'll do it also. I'm only too glad she hasn't done it already, when it began to cry—it has cried incessantly ever since it was born—and no wonder."

"Poor little soul!" said Mr. Trevena, roused into unwonted interest. He had lived so long the life of a bachelor and a bookworm that he rarely troubled himself much about external things—human things—but left all that to his wife. "I think we had better tell Mrs. Trevena: she will be sure to know what you ought to do."

"Yes—but not yet. Don't spoil her pleasure. Look! I am sure she is enjoying herself."

"My wife has the faculty of enjoying everything."

And indeed it seemed so, though just now her enjoyment was no wonder. Few could have seen unmoved those great fields of snow, rising upwards into gigantic peaks, white as no fuller on earth could whiten them—

like the robes of the righteous described in Revelations. The whole scene, in its silence, grandeur, and dazzling brightness, was liker heaven than earth. One's petty mortal life, with its trivial cares and foolish joys, sank, dwarfed into nothingness, before the majesty of those everlasting hills, covered with perpetual snow. It was the nearest image we can imagine, in this poor changing earth, of that Eternity from whence we came and into which we go.

She sat gazing with an expression full of peace, though the traces of tears were on her cheeks—so rapt, that she never noticed the approach of the two men.

"Look at her," said the American, with honest admiration written on his shrewd brown face. "By George! how pretty she must have been when she was young."

"She is pretty now—at least to me," replied the Englishman with dignity. "My dear Susannah, are you rested? Is it not time we were going home?"

"'Going to hum,' as we say—or as you English say that we say—often a very different thing," observed Dr. Franklin, trying hard to recover his equanimity and good humor.

"Which means going to our hotel; not a bad substitute for home. Madame is very kind. But oh! Austin, I shall be glad to be once again really 'at home!' We must try to move on to-morrow. So adieu—for ever, most likely—you beautiful San Gottardo!"

Smiling she rose, collected the fragments of lunch,— "They will do for these little lads who were selling edelweiss and alpenrosen beyond Hospenthal,"—and joined her companions in the carriage.

Both Mr. Trevena and Dr. Franklin were very silent on the homeward road; but Mrs. Trevena talked and smiled rather more than usual to make up for it. And they acquiesced in, or at any rate did not oppose, her plan of going down the next day to Fluelen, and thence on to Lucerne.

"So this will be our last night in the Urseren Thal; for, if you go back to America as you intend, doctor, we are none of us ever likely to be at Andermatt again."

"I earnestly hope I never may be!" said Dr. Franklin, as reaching the hotel he looked at his watch. "Half an hour past my time. Well, it doesn't matter—only—what a hullabaloo she'll make. You'll remember, sir? And I'll see you again at the *table d'hôte*—after you have told your wife."

"Told me what?"

"You needn't be alarmed, ma'am. Take a quiet evening walk—lucky comfortable couple that you are!—and your husband will explain it. Bless us—what a sunset! —Why did heaven make the outside world so beautiful, and the people in it so—— But I beg your pardon, Mrs. Trevena—Not all people—not all."

He took off his hat to her with rough respect, and disappeared toward a small *dependance* only used when the hotel was full, on the other side of the road.

Up that road, shortly afterwards, the English couple might have been seen strolling, arm-in-arm, sometimes even hand-in-hand, for those long-divided years had made them almost childlike in their wedded happiness now. They cast a glance at the *dependance* as they passed, but nothing was visible: so they slowly disappeared along the level road towards that wonderful Devil's Bridge—the chief sight of Andermatt; whence they did not return till the *table d'hôte* dinner had already begun.

It was a long walk—and a momentous one—perhaps the most momentous they had ever taken in all their placid lives. When he met them at the dinner-table, Dr. Franklin was quite sure Mr. Trevena had told his wife everything. She was very silent—even for her; she ate little; and between the many courses by which Swiss hotels so cleverly contrive to make a palatable something out of almost nothing, she fell into long reveries. Still, there was a new brightness—a pleasure amounting to rapture—in her eyes, which made her look quite young, and fairly startled the good doctor.

Dinner over, she drew him aside. "My husband has given me your message. I hardly know what to advise. But first, may I go and see that poor woman?"

"'Poor' woman, indeed! and you want to go and see her? I knew it!—just like you. But, my dear madam, you can't. She is madder—or badder—than ever. All her talk is how to get rid of the child. My impression is if you went to see her she would shut the door in your face."

"Try, nevertheless. I might do something—say something. We are both women, and"—with a quiver of the lips—"mothers—at least I have been a mother. Perhaps, poor thing! her head is a little wrong."

"Not a bit of it, unless we adopt the theory which some of my profession have started, that all badness is madness. A very comfortable doctrine, and then nobody need be punished for anything. But, ma'am, if there is a thing true in this world it is that text, 'Be sure your sin will find you out.' As I told her only tonight, you can't go against nature, but nature will have her revenge some day. However, that's no affair of mine."

"Perhaps not, yet let us try. Go and ask her if she will see me."

"Very well, ma'am."

During his absence, Mrs. Trevena sat alone—at least practically so, for her husband, according to old habit, had taken a book out of his pocket and become absorbed therein. Susannah, who did not read very much, was content to watch the great white mountains melting away in the twilight; and think—and think.

"It's no use!" said Dr. Franklin, returning. "I believe she is mad—quite mad. She will see nobody. She says the best kindness anybody could show her would be to take away the child; that children have been her bane and nuisance all her life, and she wants no more of them. When I suggested that He who sent them might require them at her hand, she laughed in my face. I think she believes in neither God nor devil."

"Poor soul! Could you not find out her friends?"

"I wish I could, but I have not the slightest clue. I can get nothing out of her, or her servant either—except that she has been living for six months in Italy."

Mrs. Trevena thought a minute. "Do you think it possible she may be the Italian prima donna who ran away from Milan? To an actress or singer children might be a hindrance—if she had no motherly heart."

"Yes—yes," said the doctor, meditating. "You women are twice as sharp as we. But she is American. Still, she may have passed under an Italian name. She declares no power on earth shall make her confess her own."

"Poor soul!" said Susannah again. "She has husband, children, home—and she hates and flies from them all. How much she is to be pitied!"

"Pitied!" cried the doctor almost angrily. "Mrs. Trevena, I think you would speak a good word for the devil himself! And truly, if there ever was a she-devil, it's that woman! I wonder what Mrs. Franklin would say to her! But I know what she'd do—she'd take home the little one, and I should have eleven young shavers to bring up instead of ten. She'd make me adopt it—as we can and often do in America."

Mrs. Trevena did not answer at first—then she said gently. "Since I cannot see the mother, do you think you could manage for me to see the baby?"

This was not quite easy, for Madame, with a creditable dread of scandal in her hotel, had managed so cleverly that no one but herself and the American doctor even knew of the existence of the hapless, unwelcome babe. And only after nightfall, when the inmates had all retired, would she consent that it should be brought for a minute or two to the door of the *dependance*, wrapped in a shawl, and carried in Dr. Franklin's arms.

Mrs. Trevena took it softly in hers, and pressed to her bosom the tiny red, puckered face.

"It is a boy, you say? Mine was a boy too. He lived just six hours." It was only a murmur, but the kind-hearted Kentuckian heard it—and understood.

"It's a fine child, ma'am; healthy and strong. No—it won't wake. Its mother has given it some sleeping stuff—she will do this, though I tell her she might as well give it poison. She'll kill it some day, if it isn't taken away from her. She says, new-born brats don't matter—they're only half-alive. You might drown them like kittens—and no harm done."

Mrs. Trevena did not answer—perhaps scarcely heard. Evidently her heart was full. She pressed her cheek, her lips, with more than tenderness—passion—to the little sleeping face.

"If mine had only lived! I had him but six hours, and yet—I can never forget him." And then either her tears, now fast falling, or the unsteady hold of her trembling hands, woke the child; who gave a little cry—that helpless infant wail, to some women so irritating, to others the unfailing key which unlocks every corner of the true motherly heart.

"I must take it back," said Dr. Franklin.

"Oh no—no—let me have it for just five minutes more—for the night perhaps—I'll take care of it. Any woman of common sense can manage a baby. Let me have it, doctor."

"I can't," replied the doctor gravely. "Ma'am, you forget. What would Mr. Trevena say?"

Mrs. Trevena resisted no more. She resigned the child, and then stood with her empty hands tightly folded, and her eyes, tearless now, fixed on the stars;

which treading their silent courses seemed so far away from human cravings and human woes. Perhaps she saw them—perhaps not, but there was a light in her eyes as bright as stars.

She said not a word but "good-night and thank you" to Dr. Franklin, when, having taken her across the road to the hotel, he left her at her own room-door; with a hearty grip of the hand—for he, too, honest man! had been not unmoved.

"Poor little brat! I wonder what will be the end of it. Well! I guess the Lord sometimes makes things mighty unlevel in this world of ours. Perhaps He does it that we may try to put them straight ourselves. We often can—if we see our way. Whew! I wish the Lord would help me to see mine."

And the good fellow—who had a habit of referring to "the Lord" pretty frequently, not with any irreverence, but in a fashion rather startling to British ears—went off to his bed, whistling, and slept the sleep of the contented and the just.

So did Mr. Trevena—in fact his wife found him asleep when she came in, and did not waken him. But she herself lay awake till dawn.

CHAPTER II.

Next morning Mr. and Mrs. Trevena sat over their early *café*, by their bedroom fire, welcome even in June at Andermatt—a comfortable couple, placid and loving; for, before returning to his book, he stooped and kissed her affectionately.

"You'll be busy over your packing, my dear, for we really will start to-morrow, if I get the letters and some money to-day. Dr. Franklin will share our carriage to Fluelen; he can surely leave his patient now. By the bye, did you see the baby last night?"

"Yes;" and coming closer she laid her hand on her husband's arm, and her head on his shoulder. "Can you give me a few minutes, Austin, my dear?"

"A hundred if you like, my darling. Is it to speak about the journey? Well, we shall soon be safe at home, and oh! how glad we shall be."

"Very glad. But—it is an empty home to come back to."

"How do you mean?—Oh yes—I see. My poor Susannah! You should not have gone and looked at that baby."

He spoke very tenderly—more so than might have been expected from his usually formal and absent manner.

She gave one little sob, then choked it down, put her arms round his neck and kissed him several times. An outsider might have smiled at the caresses of these two elderly people; but love never grows old, and they had loved one another all their lives.

"Don't mind my crying, Austin. Indeed, I am happy, quite happy. Yesterday, when I sat under the wall of snow, and looked at the beautiful sights all round me, I thought how thankful I ought to be—how contented with my lot—how blessed in my home and my husband. And I ceased to be angry with God for having taken away my baby."

"Poor Susannah!—poor Susannah!"

"No, rich Susannah! And so, I determined to grieve no more—to try and be happy without a child. But now——"

"Well, my darling?"

"Austin, I think God sometimes teaches us to renounce a thing, and when we have quite renounced it, gives it back to us, in some other way."

"What do you mean?"

She tried to speak—failed more than once—and then said, softly and solemnly, "I believe God has sent that child, whom its mother does not care for, to me—to us. Will you let me have it?"

Intense astonishment and bewilderment was written on every line of Mr. Trevena's grave countenance.

"God bless my soul! Susannah, what can you be thinking of?"

"I have been thinking of this and nothing else, ever since you told me what Dr. Franklin told you. From that minute I felt the child was meant for me. Its mother throws it away; she does not care a straw for it —whilst I—oh Austin—you don't know—you don't know!"

She pressed her hands upon her childless breast, as if to smother down something that was almost agony.

"No, my dear," Mr. Trevena answered dryly; "I can't be expected to know. And if you were not such a very sensible woman I should say that you don't know either. How can respectable old folk like us encumber ourselves with a baby—a waif and a stray—a poor little creature that we know nothing on earth about?"

"But God does," she answered solemnly. "Listen, Austin. When I was a very little girl I picked up a bit of sweetwilliam—trodden under foot and nearly dead. My playfellows laughed at me, and said it would never grow; but I planted it and it did grow—it grew into the finest root in my garden. An omen, I think; for I have done the same thing several times afterwards in the course of my life, and—my sweetwilliams always grew! Let me try one more."

"My dear, you would coax a bird off a bush. But what on earth do you want to do? To buy a baby? The woman will not give it—she wished to sell it, you know. Twenty pounds is her price. I really haven't that much about me."

"Don't jest, dear." And when he saw the expression of his wife's face, Mr. Trevena felt it was no jesting matter. He had ever been a man of one idea, or rather of two ideas—his books and his Susannah; every corner of his heart was filled up by either the one or the other. Perhaps he had felt a natural pang when his hope of fatherhood was quenched, but the regret soon died out, and his life became complete as before. Love of offspring is with men more a pride than an affection; at least till the children are intelligent human beings. The passionate craving which made the Hebrew mother cry, "Give me children or else I die," is to them absolutely unknown. Nor, as a rule, does a man take much interest in any children not his own. But with a woman it is different.

Susannah sat down, for she was trembling too much to stand. Austin saw it, and his heart melted.

"Come, don't fret, my love, and we will consider the matter. But—think of the trouble a baby would be."

"I will take it upon myself. I know I can."

"Then again, our income is so small—too small to bring up and provide for a child."

"We should have had to do it for our own, had he lived."

"Then—there is my brother Hal."

Mrs. Trevena's sweet face hardened a little—it could not but harden. This scamp of an elder brother had been to the younger one a torment, a disgrace, ever since their college days; also a ceaseless drain, hindering his prospects and delaying his marriage. Family pride—it scarcely could be called family affection—had prevented the good clergyman from throwing off this horrible incubus, until he got a living and married his Susannah, whose strength had in some degree counteracted his weakness, taught him to say No, and proved to him that to sustain a bad man in his badness, even though he be your own flesh and blood, is not a virtue, but a weakness.

"I thought we had done with Hal when you paid his passage out to Australia."

"Ay, but he may come back again—he often does," said the husband, with a weary look. "He has turned up, you know, from all the ends of the earth, to worry me as much as ever."

"But that was when you had not me beside you. Now——"

"I know—I know. Would that I had had you beside me years ago!"

As perhaps, but for Hal, and a certain weakness, not seldom combined with an affectionate nature, he might have had. But his wife said nothing—except to notice that Dr. Franklin was walking outside.

"Shall we call him in and speak to him?"

"About the baby? Have you so set your heart upon it, Susannah? Am not I enough for you? Would you be like Hannah, the wife of Elkanah?"

"Hannah prayed, and God sent her her little Samuel. Who knows but that He may in His own mysterious way have sent me mine?"

She spoke in a whisper—solemn and tender. Her voice was so entreating, her expression so rapt—as if she saw farther than any but herself could see—that the good kind husband resisted no more. Though he did not always understand her, he had an instinct that whatever his Susannah did was sure to be right. It was always difficult to him to say No to anybody, but to say No to her was quite beyond his power.

"Well—well, we will at least consider the matter. Let us do as you say—call in Dr. Franklin and talk it over."

The talk lasted a long time, without eliciting any new facts or coming to any satisfactory conclusion. Dr. Franklin was less surprised at Mrs. Trevena's Quixotic idea, as her husband called it, than an Englishman would have been; he said the adoption of children was a not uncommon thing in America.

"Indeed, I have often advised it as an absolute duty to rich and childless people, who wished to make themselves happy with young life about them, and avoid a selfish, useless old age. A child in the house helps to educate everybody in it. Not that Mrs. Trevena needs much education," added he, with blunt courtesy, "but it would make her happy and do her good; and, as the Bible says, she would 'save a soul alive.'"

"What! save a child by taking it from its parents? That is not according to the Bible," answered the perplexed clergyman.

"I am sorry to say, sir, that there are lots of children in this world who can only be saved by taking them from their parents. This poor little wretch is one. He is a fine, healthy, perfect child—splendid physiological and phrenological developments—might make a grand fellow, if anybody could protect him from the woman that bore him; who doesn't deserve the blessing of a child. Your wife does. I think with her—that the Lord sent it to her."

Mrs. Trevena lifted up to him grateful eyes, but said nothing.

"It seems so ridiculous, and yet so horrible—the idea of buying a child," said Mr. Trevena. "Besides, we should have all the responsibility of it, and no legal rights whatever."

"There we have the advantage of you." The Kentuckian drew himself up to his full long length, and spoke—more nasally than ever, it must be owned—but with an honest warmth that neutralized all national peculiarities. "In my country, where every man stands on his own feet, where we have neither the curse of primogeniture nor the burden of hereditary rank, any respectable person, or any married couple, agreeing together, can legally adopt a child."

Mrs. Trevena looked up eagerly. "How?"

"By presenting a petition to one of our courts of law, and after due examination of the parents, if alive and deserving, and of the child, if old enough, obtaining a decree of adoption, which is called 'the muniment of title.' This makes it the adopting parents' lawful heir, and the real parents have no more right over it, which is, in some cases, a great blessing. It was in two, I know of—one an orphan, the other worse. Both children were adopted —and both saved—as I only wish somebody would save this poor little soul. It's a great mystery, Mrs. Trevena, but sometimes the Lord seems to send children to those who don't deserve them, and not to those that do. Many miserable little creatures have I seen, who might have been seized and saved, body and soul—as I managed to save those two—— But I beg your pardon. I go talking on—interrupting your husband at his letters —for I see he has got them at last."

There were only two—but evidently important—for Mr. Trevena had dropped out of the conversation at sight of them, and sat poring over the first one; till coming to the end he uttered something almost like a cry. His wife came to him.

"What is the matter?"

"Oh, nothing. Only Hal wanting money—as usual. And why, do you think?" There was a mixture of the pathetic and the ludicrous in Mr. Trevena's face as he looked up. "He is married!—actually married this time—to a girl twenty years younger than himself."

Mrs. Trevena's anxious face grew hard and stern. "It is the maddest—not to say the baddest—thing he has ever done. Who is she?"

"An Australian—Colonial born.—Hal's wife! and we know nothing on earth about her."

"And she probably knows nothing on earth about him—which is worse. Poor soul!"

Here Dr. Franklin, feeling he had unawares come upon a family skeleton, was discreetly slipping away.

"Stay a minute," said Mrs. Trevena, "if you will pardon this discussion of our family correspondence. Austin, open the other letter. It may be our money from home, and then we can arrange with Dr. Franklin for our departure to-morrow."

There was a sad sort of resignation in her tone, as of a woman who has all her days been accustomed to give up everything she most cared for, and make the best of what was left—eating the crumbs and not the festival meats of life. But no one knows what Fate is bringing. The other letter her husband opened listlessly—and almost dropped out of his hands with a look of amazement and joy.

"Susannah—O Susannah! it has come at last!"

"What, dear?"

"The living—that college living I have been hoping for these twenty years!—It is offered me now.—No more poverty—no more struggle. My Susannah will be a well-to-do woman for the rest of her days. Thank God—thank God!"

Quite overcome, Mr. Trevena sat down, covering his eyes with his hand. His wife, forgetful of the stranger's presence, knelt down beside him in silence. By their deep joy the doctor could plumb the depth of their past suffering, hitherto so well concealed. He walked to the window, unwilling to walk quite away, and contemplated Juno, the big St. Bernard, with three gigantic puppies gamboling round her.

"A mother of sons is a fine sight, be it brute or woman," said he to himself, *à propos* of nothing; and gazed silently on till he felt a gentle touch on his arm.

"You are so kind—you will rejoice with us. My husband has just got a new living—the very prettiest rectory in all Cornwall. We are not such poor people now, as we told you we were this morning."

"The Lord be thanked! His ways are not so unlevel after all, if one only waits to see," said the Kentuckian, with his own rough but unmistakable devoutness, as he shook hands with both his friends, and congratulated them sincerely. "And now," said he, with his usual directness,—"about the child."

"What child?" said Mr. Trevena absently.

"The baby your wife wants to adopt, and I hope she may. I'll help her to do it, with your permission. You can afford now to give yourselves a son and heir."

"But—Susannah, what would Hal say?"

There is a saying that "the worm will turn." Mrs. Trevena had never been a "worm"; but she had been a much-enduring woman—till now. It was the crisis of her patience. Endurance changed into resistance. She rose up, and even Dr. Franklin was startled by the fire in her eyes.

"I think, husband, it does not matter two straws what Hal says. He has spent all his own patrimony and yours. You have maintained him for years; now he has chosen to marry, and it is the maddest if not the wickedest thing he ever did in his life—which is saying a good deal. He has no further claim upon you—upon us. Let him go."

Rarely did Mrs. Trevena speak so much or so fiercely. That last "Let him go!" fell hard and sharp as the knife which has to cut off something corrupt, obnoxious—and does it, with a righteous remorselessness better than any feeble pity, which is often only another name for self-ease. Even as there are many people, who are benevolent only to give themselves pleasure, so there are many more who are merciful only to save themselves pain.

"She is right," said Dr. Franklin, dropping his bony hand heavily on the table as a sort of practical amen to the discussion. "Since you have let me into your family secrets, excuse me, sir, if I use the freedom of saying, your wife is right. There are limits, even to the claims of flesh and blood. Let your brother go his way; and do you take the child which the Lord sends you, bring it up as your son, and trust to His making it a real son to you both in your old age. Nobody can look ahead; but at any rate you will make your wife happy, and, as I said, you will save a soul alive."

He waxed preternaturally eloquent, as he stood, honest man! his long lean figure drawn up to its full height; his arms folded and his keen eyes glittering—was it with that tender pity which only the strong can feel? or the generous indignation that only the righteous can show? Anyhow, his words, so cordially in earnest, had their effect.

Mr. Trevena turned to his wife. "Susannah, do you really wish this?"

"Yes, Austin, I do."

"Then I consent. For my wife's sake, Dr. Franklin."

"And for His sake," added Susannah, with an upward glance of her sweet eyes—eyes that had in them the perpetual light from heaven, which a man might thankfully and safely follow all his life through. "He says to us, Take this child and nurse it—*for Me.*"

"And now," said the doctor, clearing his throat, and sticking his hat fiercely down over his brows—"I'll go and see about this business—the oddest bit of business I ever came across. I've bought a good many things—but I never yet bought a baby. What form of receipt will the woman want, I wonder? And she must sign her name to it—which will let us know what her name is—for I haven't the slightest idea. By Jove! she's a queer customer; the most unwomanly woman I ever had to do with. Still—I'll face her. Here goes!"

He gave his soft felt hat another bang, which left it crooked on his head; and soon they saw him striding off to the *dependance*. They felt that, spite of his address and *brusquerie*, if there was ever a man fit to be trusted with a troublesome business, and certain to carry it through, it was the long Kentuckian.

Hour after hour the day went by. Husband and wife did not talk much; neither was given to talking—their long-parted lives had been too solitary: besides they understood one another so well that discussion was unnecessary. Even at this great crisis, when both had plenty to think about, they kept a mutual tender silence; and as they took their quiet daily walk together, spoke of the mountains, the flowers, and all other things about them which they were accustomed to notice and take pleasure in—the placid pleasure in nature's blessings which grows rather than decreases with years. But they never once referred either to Hal and his marriage, or to the transaction which Dr. Franklin was engaged in at the *dependance* close by.

As they passed it on their return it was as silent as death; the doors and windows closed, as had been the case all along. Mrs. Trevena gave a little sigh. But her husband never seemed to notice anything.

The glowing June day was beginning to melt into the long twilight of the mountains, behind whose tops the sun disappears so soon; when Dr. Franklin's knock was heard at their door. Mrs. Trevena opened it with an eager face, in which hope seemed to struggle with patience—the patience of a woman long accustomed to disappointment.

The shrewd doctor saw this at once, and held out his hand with a smile.

"Well, ma'am, congratulate me. I think I've managed it—and her. But she is the queerest fish; a 'woman of genius,' she calls herself, and not to be judged like other women. Bless my soul!—if she is a woman of genius I'm glad Mrs. Franklin isn't!—But to our business. Your hear me, Mr. Trevena?"

"Yes—yes," said the good clergyman, closing his book, but looking rather bored as he did so.

"This lady—queer as she is, I am sure she is a lady, well-educated and all that—says you may have her baby for twenty pounds English money, paid down; and that then 'the sooner you take the brat away the better.'—Those were her words. She promises never to trouble you about it—she doesn't even want to hear your name —which, indeed, I have taken the precaution not to tell her—and she refuses to tell you hers. She says you may call the boy anything you like. 'He's the image of his father—and that's why I hate him!' she said one day. Oh, she's an awful woman."

"Is he"—the color rose in Mrs. Trevena's matron cheek, but she forced herself to ask the question—"is he —do you think—his father's lawful child?"

"I conclude so. She speaks sometimes of 'my fool of a husband,' and 'the little wretches at home.' But, as I told you, I know absolutely nothing. You might as well squeeze water out of a stone as any commonsense truth out of that woman. She is a perfectly abnormal specimen of her sex."

"Perhaps she is mad."

"Not a bit of it: perfectly sound in mind and body—has made a wonderfully quick recovery. A shrewd person too—wide-awake to her own interests. If you want the baby to-morrow, she insists upon having the twenty pounds paid down to-night."

Mr. Trevena looked perplexed, and turned appealingly to his wife—as he seemed in the habit of doing in most emergencies.

"We have not got the money," she said simply. "We have hardly any money left; but our remittances will be sure to come to-morrow. If I might have the baby——"

"I wish to heaven you had it now, ma'am—for I don't want to have to give evidence to the Swiss government in a case of child-desertion, or child-murder. However, I'll go over again and see what can be done. There is the *table d'hôte* bell. Shall we go down to dinner?"

They dined, rather silently, amidst the clatter of a party of Germans who had just come up from Lucerne, and were passing on over the St. Gothard next day; and who, with characteristic economy, appealed to the "rich English" to take their carriage back, and to save them the expense of paying for the return journey.

"We might have done it, had our money come in time," said Mr. Trevena. "I am sure I don't want to stay a day longer in Andermatt than I can help."

"Nor I," added Dr. Franklin—then catching Mrs. Trevena's anxious eyes—"But I shall make it a point of honor—medical honor—to see my patient safe through. Not that she is a paying patient, though she did one day offer me a diamond ring—I am almost sorry I refused it, or it might have been some clue. "But no!"—continued he in a whisper to Mrs. Trevena—"Mother—take your son—if I can get him for you—and forget he ever had any mother besides yourself."

Once again the childless woman's eyes flashed upon the good doctor a look of passionate gratitude. Then she rose, and went and sat patiently in the window recess of the now empty *salle à manger;* watching the full round moon, risen long since, but only now appearing over the tops of the mountains—like a joy found late in life, yet none the less a complete and perfect joy.

Before long, she heard Dr. Franklin's long striding step and cheery voice.

"Well, ma'am, I've done it at last. You will get your baby. Not to-night—she 'can't be bothered' to-night, she says—but to-morrow morning. Also, I've spoken to Madame (whom I had to take into our confidence, for she threatened to turn adrift 'Madame L'Anonyme,' as she contemptuously calls her, within twelve hours), and she will sell you the clothes she lent, and the goat; or get you a *nourrice* from the next canton, so that you can keep the matter as secret as you choose."

"Thank you," Mrs. Trevena said. "But I had rather not keep it secret. I have considered everything, and I am sure it will be better to tell the plain truth at once; that I have adopted a deserted child, and that he is henceforth my son—and I am his mother."

The intonation of the last word startled even the good doctor, who knew human nature so well. It indicated one of those natures to whom motherhood is not merely a sentiment or a duty, but a passion. He felt that he had done well—or rather that heaven had done better.

"You are right," he said, "the outside world need never know any more than that—and I earnestly hope you never will either. As for the boy himself, when he grows up you may tell him as much or as little as you please."

"I shall tell him everything. The truth is always best."

Dr. Franklin shook her warmly by the hand. "I wish every boy in the world had a mother like you. May he live to 'rise up and call you blessed!'"

Middle-aged and practical folk as they were, tears stood in the eyes of both. They understood one another.

"And now," continued the doctor, "I'll just have to face that woman once more—about ten to-morrow forenoon, she said. But I shall not try to worm anything more out of either her or her servant, who obeys her like a slave—she was her slave, and foster-mother as well—you anti-slavery folk don't know the dogged fidelity of our Southern niggers. But I'll wash my hands of both —when I get the baby. And then we three—with the young 'un and the goat, or a bottle of goat's milk—will go on to Fluelen in that carriage the Germans had. I told the woman this; and oh! how she pricked up her ears, as if the only thing she wished was to get rid of her baby and never see it again in this world—as I fervently hope she never may!"

"I hope so too; and I intend it," said Mrs. Trevena, very quietly, but with a firmness that betrayed the possible "iron hand in velvet glove"—even her little hand. And as Mr. Trevena just then lounged in—with his gentle, gentlemanly, absent manner, and his eternal book under his arm—Dr. Franklin thought that perhaps the little woman had found out how in this life firmness is as necessary as gentleness.

Everybody slept soundly that night; the worthy doctor because he believed he had done his duty; Mrs. Trevena because she saw plainly before her in long glad vista, hers; and Mr. Trevena, because he did not think about it at all; being absorbed in a new reading which he had hit upon of a line in Horace, and which he tried to explain to his wife before they went to sleep. During the night one of those dense white mists, common at Andermatt, swept down from the mountains; by morning everything outside the hotel had become invisible; and, after the early departure of the German tourists, the almost empty hotel seemed to become as quiet as the grave.

The post arrived, bringing Mr. Trevena his expected remittances, which he handed over as usual to his Chancellor of the Exchequer, as he called her—well for him that she was! With hands slightly trembling she examined the notes—there was enough money to take them home, and twenty pounds over.

Mrs. Trevena looked nervously at her watch. "Is not Dr. Franklin late?" she said—or rather was about to say—when she saw him hurrying in from the *dependance*.

"I want you, ma'am. Come back with me. If that woman is not a murderess, she is next door to one. But we may save the child yet if we make haste."

Mrs. Trevena threw a shawl over her head and ran. There, in the middle of the one poor room, which had witnessed its unwelcome birth, lay the deserted child, half-naked and only half-alive, for no one seemed to have taken the trouble to feed or dress it. The floor was strewn with the debris of a hasty packing, and the accumulated untidiness of many days. In the midst of this chaos the poor infant lay, moaning its little life away—a very feeble moan now, for it must have lain there several hours.

Mrs. Trevena dropped on her knees beside it. "Oh, my baby! my baby!" she cried almost with a sob; took it in her arms, pressing the stone-cold limbs to her warm breast, and wrapping it in the skirt of her dress, as she sat on the floor.

"It is mine, altogether mine now. Oh, doctor, can you save it yet?"

"I'll try," muttered the good man, as he too knelt down and felt the fluttering pulse—rapidly sinking into stillness and death.

They did try; and with the help of Madame, who arrived presently from the hotel, equally voluble in her fury against "Madame L'Anonyme," and her wondering respect for the gentle English miladi,—they succeeded. Another hour, and the fleeting life had been arrested: the danger was past; and the poor little babe, warmed, fed, and clothed, lay safe in the bosom of its new-found mother, who rejoiced over it almost as if it had been the child of her own travail, which heaven had taken away.

"This little fellow will owe you his life almost as much as if he had been born your own," said the doctor,

D

regarding them both with the curious tenderness which sometimes softened his keen, shrewd eyes. "If we had not come to the rescue, he would have been dead in another half-hour. Now—Bless us! what a pair of lungs!"

"No, he will not die—as his mother meant him to die," cried indignant Madame, who with nearly all the female servants of the hotel had gathered round in compassion and sympathy. "The barbarous woman! and, though she had a wedding-ring on her finger, I believe she was a woman of no character at all."

"We do not know that," said Mrs. Trevena, trying to understand the French, and speaking firmly in her own tongue. "Let us be silent about her. She is—or rather she was—my boy's mother."

From that hour Susannah always said, "*My* boy."

"Madame L'Anonyme" had in truth disappeared, as anonymously as she came. How she and her servant had contrived to secure the Fluelen carriage, pack up their small baggage, and make what was literally a "moonlight flitting," so quietly that no one had heard them depart, was, and remained, a complete mystery.

No one sought to unravel it. No one pursued them or cared to do so—what could be gained by it? Nothing could be got out of them. The puzzle was, how, without money, they had managed to get away; and it was not till the uproarious complaints of Madame had been a little stilled by the application of a few English shillings—or rather American dollars—that the doctor, seeing Mrs. Trevena uneasy because her part of the compact had not been fulfilled,—she had got the child, and the twenty pounds was still in her pocket—owned, blushing like a girl, that he himself had "taken the liberty" of paying it the night before.

"It seemed the only way to quiet the woman, and keep her from doing something desperate. But you see she had less of desperation and more of worldly wisdom than I thought. Anyhow she is gone, and we have got rid of her—I hope for ever."

"Thanks to you," said Mrs. Trevena, as she silently put the bank-note in the doctor's hand; and he took it, for he was a practical man, and a poor man besides.

"I have made everything as safe as I can," said he. "She has no clue to us, or we to her. Neither she nor her servant, who speaks only English, has ever heard your name—only mine; and as I am going back to America at once, she is not likely to find me out there. If she ever does, and wants to know about her child, she'll meet her match—that's all!"

"Thank you," said Mrs. Trevena. For Mr. Trevena, he said nothing at all; he only watched with benignant pleasure the unspeakable content of his wife's face; and thence glanced downwards, with a sort of amused curiosity, to the little creature on her lap, especially its hands and feet, as if to find out whether it had the right number of fingers and toes, and was no abnormal specimen of anthropology. A simple man, and a good man, was the Reverend Austin; never swerving from his one domestic creed, that if his Susannah thought a thing right, it was right.

So the exciting episode, which Madame in her anxiety for the good name of her hotel wisely hushed up as

much as possible, settled down into calmness. The
baby did not die, as its natural, unnatural mother had
probably hoped it might. The goat was an excellent
foster-mother; and before forty-eight hours were over,
Mrs. Trevena felt—ay, and looked, as if she herself had
been a real mother for years.

Dr. Franklin watched her with his expression of dry
humor, tempered by kindliness.

"Mrs. Franklin says, all the doctors and nurses going
can't manage a baby so well as one sensible woman with
a motherly heart. And as she has managed ten, maybe
she is right. Now—about the journey to Lucerne. If
you take a bottle of goat's milk with you—also a doctor,
in case of emergency, we shall get back to civiliza-
tion without any difficulty. A nice '*partie quarrée*'—
you and your husband, myself, and—this little encumbrance."

"Encumbrance!" echoed Mrs. Trevena, looking up
to Dr. Franklin with a grateful smile—no, an actual
laugh. He had never heard her laugh before. And she
had much interested him—this little woman—not merely
as a woman, but as a "case"; one of those cases which
most people disbelieve in, yet which, though rare, are
possible—a "broken heart." A disease of which, if
they have no absolute duties and are not physically
strong, women can die, without murmur or regret. They
neither struggle nor complain; but simply drop out of
life as out of a worn garment no longer worth the
wearing.

No fear of that now for Susannah. Her whole nature
seemed changed. Hope seemed to have come into her

heart—the hope that comes with young life, rising up to renew and carry on the life which had seemed fading away. Her very face grew youthful; with a look not unlike some of Raffaelle's Madonnas; far away, as if peering into the dim future; and yet content in the present—the small limited present, from day to day, and hour to hour, as mothers learn to look.

For she was a mother now to all intents and purposes. She kept saying to herself involuntarily that line of Mrs. Browning's lovely poem, "A child's grave at Florence"—

"*My* little feet, *my* little hands,
And hair of Lily's color."

As she almost persuaded herself it was; that the hair—quite wonderful for a baby a week old, which she admired and toyed with, was exactly the same shade as that on the nameless little head which had been buried, one sad midnight, in a corner of the churchyard by the vicarage garden-gate.

Often it really seemed to her that her lost child had come back alive, bringing with him the future of bliss to which she had looked forward, all through those mysterious months—and then had to renounce for ever. It revived again now. Every time she kissed the crumpled-up mottled face—which had no beauty for any one but her—she saw in imagination the face of *her son*, as boy, youth, man; carrying her forward five, ten, twenty years—years full of hope;—does not some poet call a child "a perpetual hope?"

"Think what our new home will be—a house with a child in it?" she said to her husband once; only once, for her happiness lay too deep to be talked about, even to him. Nor could he have understood it. He was not of an imaginative turn of mind. So that nothing troubled him in the present—and his wife took good care of that —he never troubled himself about the future. Like many another contented bookworm, he rarely saw an inch beyond his own nose. Yet he was the most patient and easily satisfied of men, even to remaining a day or two longer at Andermatt; and going about with Dr. Franklin instead of his wife, whose new-found duties, added to the ordinary traveling cares, which always fell upon her, not him, absorbed her entirely.

But at last the two men, coming home from a quiet wander through the flowery meadows beside the Reuss, and an investigation, chiefly to kill time, of the little chapel, with its strange glass tomb of the mummied knight lying "in his habit as he lived"—found Mrs. Trevena sitting, oblivious of Alps and antiquities, with her baby asleep on her lap, and everything settled for their departure to-morrow.

"It will soon seem all like a dream," she said, as she cast her eyes absently on the wonderful view from the window—the great circle of mountains, the georgeously colored pastures, and the wild rapid Reuss glittering in the sun. "We are never likely to see this place again; but I think I shall always remember it—the place where my boy was born."

"And born again—if one may say it without irreverence," added Dr. Franklin, "otherwise he had better be dead—as he certainly would have been now, except for you. By the bye, you will have to give the young scamp a name—and the sooner you do it the better. Get him christened, and keep a copy of the baptismal certificate. It may be useful yet. And I think you might as well make me his godfather, because I at least know when and where he was born. It will be a certain protection both to him and to you."

"Thank you!" said Mrs. Trevena gratefully—but she smiled at the idea of her child's needing "protection"—or she either. With him in her arms she felt as strong, as fearless, as any natural mother—even beast or bird, does, with the instinct of maternity upon her.

Dr. Franklin stuck to his point, insisting that a baptismal certificate was the nearest approach they could make to giving the child "a local habitation and a name" in this perplexing world, the god-parents attesting the place and date of birth, though they could only add "parentage unknown."

"And then you must take your chance as to the future, and this poor little fellow also; unless you will come with me to America, where, in our enlightened States, you can lawfully adopt him."

"But that would be of no use in England, you said, and England must be our home. Yes, we must take our chance," she added, with an undertone that implied one who meant to control chance, rather than succumb to it. "And now, about the name—the Christian name. For surname, he will take ours—shall he not, Austin?"

"Anything you like—anything you like, my dear."

"Yes, I think you are right, Mrs. Trevena. Poor little man, his name matters little. He will have to go through life as nobody's child."

"Except God's—and mine."

And Susannah pressed her lips, as solemnly as if it had been a sacrament or a vow, on the tiny hand with its curled-up fingers; the feeble right hand, so helpless now —but would it be always so?

Dr. Franklin smiled, kindly, paternally, on the creature whose life he had helped to save; why, or to what end, who could tell? All child-lives are a mystery, but this was a mystery above all. The little thing lay sleeping in unconscious peace on its adopted mother's lap: the infant who would be a man when they were in their graves. But the two men did not understand. The woman did.

Mrs. Trevena at last looked up. A twilight glow reflected from the mountains was on her face; and an inward glow, which made her almost pretty again—almost young.

"I have thought of a name. We are Cornish born, as I told you, Dr. Franklin. When I was a girl, my one hero was our great Cornishman, who was also 'Nobody's child'—found by Merlin, they say, as a little naked baby on the shore at Tintagel, but who grew up to be the stainless knight—the brave soldier—the Christian king. My boy shall do the same—in his own way. It does not matter how he was born, if he lives so that everybody will mourn him when he dies. So he shall have my hero's name. He shall be my 'King' Arthur."

"You romantic little woman!" said her husband, half apologetically, half proudly. But he listened to her, as he always did; and her decision carried the day.

Next morning, when the sun had just risen above the mountains, and was only beginning to warm the silent valley, the little party left Andermatt; Mr. and Mrs. Trevena, Dr. Franklin, and the "encumbrance," as the doctor called it, but who slept so calmly as to be no encumbrance at all. It was evidently an infant of placid mind, able to accommodate itself to circumstances.

They were followed by the benedictions and good wishes of Madame and the hotel people, who could not, to the last, understand the affair, but set it all down to English eccentricity. They departed, and the little remote Alpine Valley, which had witnessed so much, knew them no more.

CHAPTER III.

ARTHUR FRANKLIN TREVENA—for they had given him also the name of his good godfather, who parted from him at Lucerne, never probably to behold him again—"King" Arthur arrived at the vicarage with his adopted parents, creating no small sensation in the parish which they had left, a forlorn and childless couple, six months before. But the villagers were simple folks, who accepted the baby upon his "mother's" own simple statement. Mrs. Trevena was among the few people who have courage to believe that the plain truth is not only the wisest but the safest thing—that he was a deserted child, whom she had taken for her own, and meant to bring up exactly as her own. And those other mothers who remembered her sad looks when she went away, and compared them with her happy looks now, agreed that "the parson's wife" had done right and best, not only for herself, but most likely for "the parson" also.

The only individual who ventured to question this, or in any way to criticise the proceeding, was a neighboring clergyman, a college friend, who in Mr. Trevena's absence had undertaken the care of the hundred souls his parish contained. This gentleman, a man of fortune and family, remonstrated, in a letter of sixteen pages, with his "reverend brother" on what he had done, in bringing a nameless child, possibly the offspring of sin and shame, into a respectable and above all a clergyman's household. He quoted many texts, such as "the sins of the fathers shall be visited on the children," and "the seed of evil-doers shall never be renowned," which for a moment staggered the simple-minded vicar. And he ended by asking, "What would the Trevenas say?"—forgetting that the only Trevena left was Hal at the Antipodes, of whom even his old college acquaintance would have owned, if questioned, that the less said about him the better.

But, except this lengthy epistle, which Mr. Trevena read in silence, and passed on to Mrs. Trevena, by whose gleaming eyes he saw that the silence had better be continued, for there was a dangerous light in them that few men would have cared to face,—the couple met with no opposition or comment on what they had done or what they meant to do. The nine days' wonder settled down; and after the village mothers had come to look at the baby, and pronounced it the finest baby that ever was seen, everybody seemed to take the matter as quite natural. Poor people are often so kind, sometimes so romantically generous, about other people's children: many a nursing mother will not scruple to take to her home and her breast some motherless babe; and many a nameless infant, paid for at first, and then forsaken, has been brought up for charity by its foster-parents. So the fact of an adopted child did not strike these innocent villagers as anything remarkable. They only thought it was "uncommon kind" of Mrs. Trevena, and hoped she would be rewarded for her "charity."

Charity! She laughed at the word. Charity had nothing at all to do with it. A child in the house!—it was a joy incarnate—a blessing unspeakable—a consolation without end. She did her duties, neither light nor few, but through them all she hugged herself in her secret bliss. She used to think of it as she walked—as she chatted to her neighbors—and (oh sinful Susannah!) often as she sat in church. "*My* little feet—*my* little hands." When she came back to them, when she ran upstairs to the small attic—small but sunshiny—where Manette and Arthur were installed, and taking the baby, sat, rocking him and singing to him in the old-fashioned rocking-chair which had been her mother's, every care she had—and she had some, a few mole-hills that many another woman would have made into mountains—seemed to melt away. That morbid self-contemplation, if not actual selfishness, which is so apt to grow upon old maids and childless wives—upon almost all women who have arrived at middle age without knowing the " baby-fingers, waxen touches," which press all bitterness out of the mother's breast—vanished into thin air. It could not exist amidst the wholesome practicality of nursery life; a nursery where the mother is a real mother, and sees to everything herself, as was necessary in this case. For Manette, the young Swiss orphan whom they had found at Lucerne and installed as nurse, was a mere girl, who spoke no English, though she soon taught her mistress to speak French. They two became very happy together, guarding with mutual care, and sometimes just a spice of jealousy, the little warm white bundle which contained a sentient human being—or what would be one day—Manette's pet and plaything, Mrs. Trevena's "perpetual hope."

Had she been a disappointed woman? Perhaps; in some sense all women of imaginative temperament are. They start in life expecting the impossible, which of course never comes; and at last find themselves growing old with their hearts still painfully young—it may be, a little empty; for not even the best of men and husbands can altogether fill the void which Nature makes; even as no woman can fill, or ought to fill, that sterner half of a man's being which is meant for the world and its work.

But now Susannah's empty heart was filled—her monotonous life brightened; the future (she was only just over forty, and had a future still)—stretched out long and fair; for it was not her own—it was her son's. The evening before they left the vicarage for the new rectory—a sweet September evening—since it had taken fully three months to make the new home ready to receive them—she went out alone and planted a young tree, a seedling sycamore, which no one was likely to notice till it grew a tree—in the churchyard corner, where was the little grave of which nobody knew. But she scarcely felt it a farewell. She thought how the fibres would wrap themselves tenderly round the buried bones, and the top would spread itself out into green leaves and branches. And it seemed as if out of her dead baby's grave had sprung the other child—another and yet the same—sent direct from heaven to be her comfort and blessing. Unconsciously she repeated to herself the benediction of the Psalmist—

"He shall be like a tree planted by the water-side,

that will bring forth his fruit in due season; his leaf also shall not wither; and look! whatsoever he doeth it shall prosper."

"It will be so," she said to herself, "if I have strength to bring him up in the right way, to make him into a just man—'a man that feareth the Lord.' Then, I need have no fear. 'Whatsoever he doeth it shall prosper.'"

And little Arthur—somehow, from the first, he was always called Arthur, never "baby"—did seem to prosper: as much in his new home as in his old one. He had a larger and better nursery, not at the top, but at the end of the house; which was a very pretty house, the prettiest as well as the most comfortable that Susannah had ever lived in. From her youth up she had had to battle with the domestic ugliness that accompanies grinding poverty; to smother down her tastes and predilections, to live in streets instead of fields—at least till her marriage. And even marriage had brought little respite in the hard work, the ceaseless cares—inevitable from the necessity of making sixpence do the work of a shilling.

But now all was changed. She had as much money as she needed—enough even to lay by a little (oh! joyful economy!) for the future education of her son.

"We cannot provide for him," she had said to her husband, "but we can give him a good education, and then let him work for himself. It is the best thing for all boys. It might have been better for Hal" (she thought, but did not say, perhaps also for Hal's brother) "if he had been thrown upon the world without a single halfpenny."

So when she saw the pretty rectory nestling under its

acacia tree beside the lovely old church, and knew there was income enough to live there comfortably, she yet determined to waste nothing; to expend nothing foolishly upon outward show, or in "keeping up a position"—as the owners of the great house close by were reported to have done for generations. Consequently, the Damerels of the last generation had been too poor to occupy their splendid abode—or even to come back to it—except to be buried. Their vault in the old church was all that remained to them, in spite of their ancient name, and an estate which had belonged to them for centuries. Her boy, Susannah often thought, blossoming day by day into rosy infancy—the darling of his good Manette and his devoted "mother"—was happier than the heir of all the Damerels—a poor idiot, report said, never seen or heard of, whose family home was let, and the property put into Chancery, until his fortunate death cleared the way for some distant cousins, ready to fight over the title and estate like dogs over a bone.

"So much for 'family'—so much for 'fortune!'" meditated Mrs. Trevena; and was almost glad that she herself was the last of her race, and that her husband's only relation was Hal—safe away in Australia. "You will start in life all free, my darling—as free as if you had dropped from heaven in a basket. You will stand on your own feet, and make your own way in the world, with nobody to hamper you, and torment you—except your mother!"

And she kissed with a passion of tenderness the baby eyes, which had already begun to develop intelligence, and the sweet baby mouth, so smiling and content; for

Arthur, like most healthy and carefully reared children, was an exceedingly "good" child—who gave little trouble to any one. Before the winter was over he had learnt to know his mother's step and voice, to laugh when she entered the nursery and to cry when she left it. Soon, if brought face to face with a stranger, he would turn away, clasp his little fat arms tight round her neck and hide his face on her shoulder, as if recognizing already that she was no stranger, but his natural protector, refuge, and consolation—his mother, in short, and everything that a mother ought to be.

For his father—well! young infants scarcely need one; and certainly the father does not need them—often quite the contrary. But it rather pleased Mr. Trevena to be called "papa"—as they decided he should be; and now and then, when he met Manette walking in the garden with Arthur in her arms, he would stop her, and, stroking with one finger the rosy cheek, remark that it was "a very nice baby." But he did not investigate or interfere further. Even had it been his own child, he probably would have done no more. A baby was to him a curious natural phenomenon, which he regarded with ignorant but benevolent eyes, much as he did the chickens in his farmyard, or the little pigs in his sty; but taking no individual interest in them whatever. Not until the spring had begun and the leaves were budding and the primroses springing about Tawton Magna, making it truly what it was said to be, the prettiest rectory in all Cornwall—did Manette report that "Monsieur" had actually kissed "*le bébé*"—that it had crowed to him and pulled his hair, and altogether conducted itself with an intelligence and energy worthy of nine or even ten months old.

"Is it really nearly a year since we were in Switzerland?" said Mr. Trevena to his wife, as she joined him at the gate; she always went his parish rounds with him, and did everything for him, exactly as before the coming of little Arthur; only her many solitary hours were solitary now no more. But to her husband everything was made so perfectly the same that he often forgot the very existence of the baby. "Arthur—that is his name, I think—really does credit to you, my dear—and the rectory too. It must be a very healthy house, for I never saw you look so well."

She smiled. They loved one another very dearly—those two; old as they were—and different in many ways. But difference of character does not prevent affection—rather increases it sometimes.

"All the village tells me what a fine child Arthur is—the first child, by the bye, that has been in the rectory for fifty years. My predecessor, as you know, was an old bachelor. Everybody is delighted to have a lady in the village. You and your boy bid fair to be the pets of the parish, Susannah, my dear."

Which was true—and not unnatural. For her motherly heart, warmed through and through with the sunshine of happiness, opened not only to her own, but to every child she came near; to every poor soul, old or young, that wanted happiness and had it not. Everybody liked her—everybody praised her; and husbands are always proud to have their wives liked and praised. The rector was very proud of his Susannah.

E

They strolled peacefully together through the village, administering ghostly counsel and advice; together with creature comforts which Mrs. Trevena held to be equally desirable. She was a capital clergyman's wife — she liked to "mother" everybody.

As usual, their walk ended in the church, which was open for its Saturday cleaning. It was a curious old building—very "tumble-down," the parish thought, but was happily too poor to have it "restored"; so it remained for the delight of archæologists, and especially of Mr. Trevena. He never wearied of examining the brasses, the old monuments, the huge worm-eaten, curiously carved pews; and especially "the Squire's pew," as large as a small parlor, where the last Damerels, the baronet and his lady, had been accustomed to sit in two huge arm-chairs over the bones of their ancestors. Their own bones were now added to the rest; and the tablet describing their virtues, with a weeping angel on each side, took its place with the recumbent crusader, and the well-ruffed Elizabethan knight, with his kneeling progeny behind him.

"What a splendid old family they must have been! Probably Norman—D'Amiral corrupted into Damerel. Ah!"—and he laid a caressing hand on the head of the noseless and footless crusader—"it is a great thing to come of a good race, and to bear an honorable name."

"Is it?" said Susannah quietly, and thought of the poor half-witted boy—the heir whom her neighbors had told her of, and then of her own boy—her nameless baby—full of health and strength and intelligence, yet without a tie in the wide world. Only he was, as she had once said, "God's child"—and hers.

He had been hers for nearly two years. She had almost forgotten—and everybody else too—that he was not really her own; even the rector himself was taking kindly to his paternity, accepting it as he did the other good things which had dropped into his mouth without his seeking—when something happened which, for the time being, shook the happy little household to its very foundations.

Mrs. Trevena, one bright June day, had put on her bonnet to go and meet her child, who had been "kidnapped" as they called it—by the large kindly plebeian family, one of the many *nouveaux riches* that conveniently step into the shoes of aristocratic poverty, who inhabited Tawton Abbas. She was passing through the churchyard into the park, idly thinking how beautiful it was, how bright her life here had grown, and what had she done to deserve it all—when she came suddenly face to face with a strange gentleman, who was apparently wandering about, trying to find his way to the rectory. He was well-dressed and well-looking; but he seemed less like an ordinary visitor than a prowler. Also, though rather a handsome man, there was something sinister in his face; he was one of those people who never look you straight in the eyes.

He stood aside as the lady passed, with a half-bow, which she acknowledged. But the instant she had passed, a vague terror seized Susannah—the one little cloud which secretly hung over her entire felicity—the fear that her treasure might be grudged her, or snatched from her, by the woman who had thrown it away? She had taken every precaution to leave behind at Andermatt no possible clue; even Madame at the hotel, though she knew the names Trevena and Franklin, knew no further address than "England" and "America." Often when she looked at her bright, beautiful boy, a spasm of fear came over her, so that she could hardly bear to let him out of her sight.

This dread took hold of her now. What if the stranger were an emissary from Arthur's unknown mother—or his father—the "fool of a husband"—whom she had so despised? At the bare idea Mrs. Trevena's heart almost stopped beating. But it was not her way to fly from an evil: she preferred to meet it—and at once. She turned back and spoke.

"You seem a stranger here. Can I do anything for you?"

"Thank you—yes, I suppose I am a stranger. I have not been in England for some years."

A likeness in the tones of the voice—family voices ofter resemble one another like family faces—startled Susannah, and yet relieved her. She was almost prepared for the "stranger's" next words.

"I am told that this is the village of Tawton Magna, and the Reverend Austin Trevena is rector here?"

"Yes."

"Then would you kindly direct me to the rectory? I am Captain Trevena, his brother."

Hal, of whom they had heard nothing since the letter received at Andermatt—Hal come back from Australia! It was a great blow, and might involve much perplexity;

but it could not strike her to the heart, as the other blow would have done, had the stranger been some one coming to claim her child. After a momentary start Susannah was herself again.

Now, it so happened that since his boyhood she had never seen her brother-in-law; who evidently did not remember her at all. At first she thought she would accept this non-recognition and pass on; but it seemed cowardly. And besides she would soon have to face him; for whatever his sudden appearance might bode, she was quite sure it boded no good. Hal's fraternal affection always lay dormant—unless he wanted something.

So, looking him straight in the eyes, but putting out no hand of welcome, she said briefly, "I am Mrs. Trevena. That is the gate of the rectory," and walked on towards Tawton Abbas.

In most families there is one black sheep—happy if only one! for the well being of the whole family depends upon its treatment of the same, treatment wise or unwise, as may happen. Few black sheep are wholly black; and some may, with care and prudence, be kept a decent gray; but to make believe they are snow-white, and allow them to run among the harmless flock, smirching every one they come near, is a terrible mistake. Perhaps Susannah sometimes recognized, with as much bitterness as her sweet nature could feel, that this mistake had all through life been made by her husband.

She knew Austin was at home, and thought it best the brothers should meet—since they must meet—quite alone; while she gathered up all her courage, all her common sense, to face the position. Captain Trevena—

as he called himself, having been in the militia once, till he was turned out—had not attempted to follow her. Perhaps he was afraid of her; or thought he had good need to be; which was true.

A kind of superstitious halo has been thrown round the heads of prodigal sons—doubtless originating in the divine parable, or the human corruption of it. Only people forget how that prodigal son, saying, "I will arise," really does arise, leaving behind him his riotous living, his husks and his swine. He goes to his father, humbled and poor, and his father welcomes and loves him. But most prodigal sons bring their husks and their swine with them, nor ever condescend to say, "I have sinned." They appear, as Hal Trevena did, as he had always been in the habit of doing—neither hungry nor naked, but quite cheerful and comfortable. They may cry "Peccavi," but it never occurs to them to forsake their sins, or to feel any more penitence than is picturesque and convenient to show.

This had been Halbert Trevena's character for the last forty years; and Susannah, suddenly meeting him after a long interval, and judging him by feminine instinct, as well as by the bitter experience of the past, did not think he was likely to be altered now.

She walked rapidly on through the pleasant, solitary park, both to calm her mind, and to consider how she was to face this emergency: which on the outside appeared nothing more than the meeting—supposed a welcome meeting—between long separated brothers. But, underneath—she knew, only too well, what it implied. And not the least of the difficulties was her good, tender-hearted husband, who, absorbed in his books, never looked ahead for a single week, and whose own nature was so sweet and simple, that he could not imagine the contrary in any human being.

Susannah hastened on with quick troubled steps, till she saw Manette and little Arthur coming down the path.

"Mammy, mammy!"—he could just say that word now, and oh, what a thrill had gone through her heart when she first heard it! Stretching out eager arms, he tried to struggle out of his perambulator and get to her—"Up, up! in mammy's arms!"

She took him up and clasped him tight—her one blessing that was all her own. More so perhaps than if he had been really her own, and had to call Hal Trevena "Uncle." As the thought smote her, involuntarily she said "Thank God!" But the clinging of his baby arms, the kiss of his baby mouth, melted the bitterness out of her heart: after a few minutes she felt herself able to return to the house, and meet whatever was required to be met there. The sooner the better, for who could tell what might be happening in her absence?

She found the two brothers sitting together in the study, looking as comfortable as if they had parted only yesterday. At least Hal did; but Austin had a troubled air, which he tried to hide under an exaggeration of ease. When his wife opened the door he looked up with great relief.

"My dear, this is Hal, from Australia. You must remember Hal, though it is so many years since you saw him."

"Twenty-four years. But half an hour ago he asked me to direct him to the rectory. He was not aware, I think, that he was speaking to the mistress of the house."

And she sat down, still without offering her hand, as if to make clear that she was the mistress of the house, and had determined to assert her position.

Captain Trevena was a shrewd man, a good deal shrewder and more quick-sighted than his brother; he too saw his position, and recognized that things might not go quite so easily with him as when the Reverend Austin was a bachelor. Still, he smiled and bowed in bland politeness.

"I am delighted to come to my brother's home, and see it adorned with a wife. I only wish I had brought mine here. Mrs. Trevena (excuse me, but as the eldest son's wife she has the first right) is a very handsome person, and our eldest son, the heir to the Trevena name, takes after her. I should have liked you to see them, Austin; but, considering all things, I thought it best to leave them both in Australia for the present."

"Of course—of course," said Mr. Trevena. Mrs. Trevena said nothing. If for a second a natural pang smote her heart, it was healed immediately. For, through the window she could see a pretty vision of Manette's blue gown, with two little fat legs trotting after it along the gravel path. She turned round, smiling—she could afford to smile.

"I am glad you are happy in your wife and son. But why leave them? What call had you to England?"

"To see my brother—was it not natural? An old *Times* fell into my hands, in which I read what (of course by some mistake) he had never told me—the presentation of the Reverend Austin Trevena to the living of Tawton Magna—value—I forget how much. So I thought I would come, just to—to congratulate him."

"A long journey for so small an object. And having accomplished it, I suppose you will return?"

"If my brother wishes it, and if he will give me a little brotherly help."

"I thought so."

Brief as this conversation was, it showed to both the brother and sister-in-law exactly where they stood. The big, hearty, well-dressed man looked across at the homely little woman, and felt that times were changed: it was war to the knife between them, and could not be otherwise.

Had he come like the proverbial prodigal, in rags and repentance, Susannah's heart might have melted. She might have killed the fatted calf, even though fearing it was in vain : she might have put the ring on his finger, though with a strong suspicion that he would pawn it the very next day. But now, when he came, fat and well-liking, yet with the same never-ending cry, like the daughters of the horse-leech, "Give, give!" she felt herself hardening into stone.

"I am sorry, but your brother's income, of which you have evidently known the extent, is absorbed by his own family and his parish. He has for years supplied you with so much that he cannot possibly do any more. He ought not."

"No, Hal," said the rector, gathering a little courage, and taking Susannah's hand as she sat beside him.

"Indeed, I ought not. You know I was telling you this before my wife came into the room."

"My husband is right," said Susannah firmly. "Therefore, Captain Trevena, all I can offer you is a night's hospitality. After that we had better part."

"My dear sister, why?"

"A man with a wife and child has no business to leave them and go wandering about the world, even for the very desirable purpose of begging money from his relations. He had better stay at home and work."

"A gentleman work!" Hal laughed; that easy, good-natured laugh which made people think him so charming. "My dear lady, it is out of the nature of things—you can't expect it. I never did work—I never shall."

"I believe you." The only thing he could say, Susannah might have added, that she did believe. He was such a confirmed liar that she began to think even the wife and child might be mythical creations, invented in order to play upon Austin's feelings.

"Nor," he continued lightly, "is there any special reason why I should work. My wife is an heiress—her father made his fortune at the gold-diggings. The old fellow dotes upon her—even more than upon me. He likes to keep her all to himself, and so makes it easy for me to run away and amuse myself."

"How comes it then that you want money?"

"My dear Miss Hyde (beg pardon, but I heard of you as Susannah Hyde for so many years that I almost forget you are anything else now), a gentleman always wants money. But it is only a temporary inconvenience. I shall be delighted to repay Austin every farthing—

with interest too, if he wishes it—as soon as ever I get back to Australia."

" And when will that be ?"

" *Cela depend.* By the bye, there is a pretty young *bonne* upon whom I was airing my French an hour ago in the road. I see her now in your garden with her ' *bébé.*' Whose child is that ?"

"Mine," said Susannah firmly.

"Yours? I thought Austin told me he had no children."

" Nor have we. This is our adopted child. We found him, and we mean to keep him and bring him up as our son."

" And heir? To inherit all you possess ?"

" What little there is left—certainly."

As Susannah spoke—slowly and resolutely—Captain Trevena's handsome face grew dark; his bland voice sharpened.

" Truly, this is a pretty state of things for a long-absent brother to come home to—a sister-in-law, not too affectionate, and an unexpected—nephew. I congratulate you, Austin, on your son. Some beggar's brat, I suppose, whom your wife has picked up in the street and made a pet of—like a stray dog or half-starved cat. What noble charity !"

" Not charity at all," answered Susannah, seeing that her husband left her to answer, as was his habit on difficult occasions. " It pleased God to take away our only child ; but He gave us this one instead. And, as I said, we mean to keep him. If we bring him up rightly, he will be the comfort of our old age."

"Indeed? But meantime a child is a rather expensive luxury—too expensive to make it possible ever to help others—your own flesh and blood, for instance. I thought, Austin, that charity began at home; and that blood was thicker than water?"

Poor Austin! he regarded his brother with that worried, badgered, perplexed look, so familiar to his face once, but which the peace of later years had almost driven away. Susannah knew it well enough; it brought back a vision of the long hopeless time of their engagement, when she was passive and powerless. But she was neither now. It was not necessary—it was not right.

"Halbert Trevena," she said, quietly enough, but with flashing eyes and glowing cheeks, "how dare you, who have been a drain upon your brother all his life—a perpetual thorn in his side and grief to his heart—how dare *you* talk of blood being thicker than water?"

"Susannah—my dear Susannah, be patient!" said the rector in a deprecating tone. "You see, Hal, we don't want to be hard upon you; but really, you seem so well off, and your wife, you say, is an heiress. We, now, Susannah and I, can only just make ends meet, I assure you."

He spoke meekly—almost apologetically. But with Susannah the day of meekness was past. "Captain Trevena, it is best to be plain with you. I am mistress of this house. I will give you a night's lodging, but nothing more. With my consent, my husband shall not waste upon you a single halfpenny. What money he has left, that you have not robbed him of, he may leave you by will; but while he lives his income is not yours—it is mine."

Sternly as it was spoken, this was the truth of the case, both in law and equity, and both brothers knew it. The cunning one shrugged his shoulders—the weak one sighed; but neither attempted to controvert it.

"Of course," said Austin at last, "one's wife is nearer than one's brother; and Susannah never speaks without having well considered everything."

"Excellent wife! Admirable marriage laws!" said Hal, tapping his boot with his cane—a very handsome silver-mounted cane. In fact, all the attire of this poor prodigal was of the most expensive kind. "'What's thine is mine, and what's mine is my own!' is a well-known saying. But I always thought, Austin, that this rule applied to us, and not to the ladies. However, *tempora mutant mores*—especially family manners. Perhaps I had better go. 'It may be for years and it may be for ever!' as the song says. Well—good-bye, Austin."

Susannah's heart softened—her husband looked so very unhappy. After all, Hal was his brother. They had been boys together; and there was still between them that external family likeness, not incompatible with the greatest unlikeness internally. The law of heredity has freaks so strange that sometimes one almost doubts its existence; yet it does exist, though abounding in mysteries capable of great modification; and above all, full of the most solemn individual warnings.

"I think you should go," said Mrs. Trevena; "but go to-morrow, not to-day. Your ways are so different from ours, that we are better apart; still, do not let us part unkindly. And carry back our good wishes to your wife and child. May you live a happy life with them, and make them happy! It is not too late."

For a minute perhaps, this man, who had never made any human being aught but miserable in all his days, felt a twinge of regret; the wing of the passing angel touched his heart—if he had one. He scanned his sister-in-law, half in earnest, as if questioning whether she was in earnest, and then the light sarcastic laugh returned. The good angel was gone.

"Oh dear, no! Not too late at all. I am the most domestic man alive. I adore my home—when I am at home. And my wife—when I can get her. But as I said, she has such a devoted papa—a millionaire—that I rarely can get her. You see, Austin?"

Austin did not see, but his wife did, and turned away; remembering bitterly that hopeless proverb about the silk purse and the sow's ear; and thinking with a vague pity of her unknown sister-in-law—the mother who had a son of her very own.

But before she had time to speak came the pattering of little feet outside, and the battering of tiny hands against the study door.

"I will leave you now," said Mrs. Trevena, rising. "You and Austin will like a chat together. We dine at two—our early dinner; we are homely people—as you see."

"But most delightful! I think I never saw such a picturesque house; or,"—as the door flew open and disclosed "King" Arthur standing there—a veritable little king—with his rosy cheeks, his cloud of curly hair, and his sturdy healthy frame,—" or a more attractive child. Come in, sir! Let me see the young interloper."

And Hal made as though he would take him in his arms, but Susannah sprang forward and took him in hers; from which safe vantage-ground the child looked out, facing the man with his honest baby eyes.

Children have strange instincts—are often wonderful judges of character. Allure as Hal might, and did, nothing would induce little Arthur to kiss him, or even let himself be touched by him. The pretty under lip began to fall; he clung to his mother, and would shortly have burst into an open cry, had not Susannah carried him away—as she wisely did—at all times when his angel-hood melted into common baby-hood. As she did so, she caught the expression of her brother-in-law's eyes, which made her clasp her little one all the closer. "King" Arthur—born amongst foes, having to be protected from his own mother, and from all his unknown kin—would, she perceived, have to be protected against one enemy more.

Glad as she was to escape, she knew she must not be absent long: she dared not. If ever man combined the serpent with the dove—the smoothest, most dainty feathered, and low-voiced of doves—it was Halbert Trevena. Many a time in old days he had wound his brother round his little finger; flattered him—cajoled him—and finally fleeced him out of every halfpenny he had. All right, of course: for were they not brothers? And have not a man's own family the first claim upon him, no matter whether they deserve it or not? So reason many excellent and virtuous folk. Are they right —or wrong?

"Poor Austin!" the wife muttered, in pity rather than in anger, as she thought of the two closeted together, and what harm might possibly ensue. And then Arthur came with his entreating "Up—up!" and the clinging of his innocent arms.

"My darling!" cried Susannah, almost sobbing. "No—blood is *not* thicker than water—unless love goes with it, and respect, and honor. My boy—my own boy!" she put back the curls and looked straight down into the pure, cloudless, infant eyes. "Be a good boy—grow up a good man—and no one will ever ask how you were born."

She allowed herself a brief rest in giving Arthur his dinner, and smiled to see how before he ate a mouthful himself he insisted on feeding the dog and the cat, and even offered a morsel to the woolly lamb—his pet plaything, which always stood on the table beside him. "The boy is father to the man;" and Susannah had already detected in her baby many a trait of character which all the education in the world could never have put into him. Even at two years old there was a natural courtesy about "King" Arthur; an instinct of tenderness to all helpless things. And Susannah was far-sighted enough to be soothed and cheered. The dread, which every mother must have with every child, lest it should not grow up as she could wish, was in her case doubled and trebled; for of necessity she was ever on the watch for hereditary qualities, mental and physical, which must be modified and guarded against. And yet, perhaps, this battle with unknown evils was not worse than the pang which some parents must feel, to see their own or others' faults reappearing in their child.

"If I were Mrs. Halbert Trevena—and my son grew up like his father!" thought Susannah, with a shudder; and almost thanked God that her child was not her own —or he might have been like his uncle.

But little Arthur—blessed child!—feared no future and no past. He was perfectly happy in his sunshiny nursery—the room in which the late rector had died, after inhabiting it for fifty years, and which the servants had been half afraid of, till the baby-voice exorcised all ghosts. There the little "King" reigned supreme, with his two dumb companions. They lived in mysterious but perfect harmony—dog, cat, and child. They played together, fed together, slept together—for often Susannah would come in and find Arthur lying on the rug with his head on the dog's neck and the cat in his arms—all three sound asleep.

It was always hard to tear herself from that pleasant room; where two years of firm control and careful love had made a naturally healthy and sweet-tempered baby into a thoroughly good child; so that his mother and Manette had rarely any trouble with him, beyond the ordinary little vagaries of childhood—the worst being a tendency to cry after "Mammy," whenever he saw her preparing to leave him—as now.

"Mammy *must* go—she *must* have her dinner, my boy; but she will come back directly afterwards. She promises!"

Already the infant mind had taken in the fact that

F

"Mammy's" promises were always to be relied on—that mammy meant what she said—and did it. And though he still could not talk much, Arthur understood every word she said, and obeyed it too; for absolute obedience was the first lesson Susannah had taught her child. The little face cleared, the detaining arms relaxed; he toddled back to his four-footed friends, and made himself quite happy. No sorrow lasts long at two years old.

But Mrs. Trevena, the instant she shut the nursery door, felt her cares leap back upon her with double fierceness. As she arranged her dress at the glass, she thought of that "very handsome person"—her sister-in-law, not in envy, but in pity; wondering what was the real truth about her and about the marriage; for all Hal's statements had to be guessed at rather than believed. He had never held facts in the least degree necessary.

She looked out into the garden, expecting to see the brothers sauntering round it, for the rector was always proud to show his garden. Well he might be: for it was a perfect picture, with its green lawn in front, its background of stately trees, and its kitchen-garden at the side—a regular old English kitchen-garden, where flowers, fruit, and vegetables all flourished together. Polyanthus and auriculas edged the beds where the young peas were rising in green rows, and the high south wall, sheltered and sunny, was one mass of peach, apricot, and nectarine blossoms. But nobody admired them—the garden was deserted. Susannah went straight to the study, and there found her husband—alone.

"Hal has just gone out, but he will be back to dinner; unless, as he says, he finds 'metal more attractive.'

Which is not likely, as he knows nobody in these parts. He came direct from London, and must go back again there—immediately."

Mr. Trevena spoke lightly, but with a certain deprecation of manner, which attracted his wife's notice.

"Immediately means to-morrow, I suppose?"

"Or perhaps to-night. Poor Hal! He is very poor, my dear. We ought to be kind to him."

"I wish to be kind to him—if he deserves it."

"He may do so. It is never too late to mend. And, my Susannah—you remember the command, 'seventy times seven.'"

Susannah, feeling almost like a wretch—a hard-hearted, unchristian wretch—clasped the long-beloved hand, generous as a child's—and often as unwise in its generosity. But that instant something aroused her suspicions.

"Why is your desk open, Austin? Shall I lock it for you? Your check-book is in it?"

"Stop a minute, dear. That check-book—Hal really had not a halfpenny, though his remittances from Australia are due next week. He will repay me—I am sure he will; so I gave him a small sum—you won't mind, dear? It was very little."

"How much?"

"Only twenty pounds."

"Twenty-five pounds was all we had in the bank; and it will be six weeks before our next dividends are due."

This was all Susannah said—what good was it to say anything more? But she dropped her husband's hand

and sat down, in passive acquiescence to fate. The old thing all over again! the same quiet endurance, but none the less the same bitter, resentful pain. All the bitterer that there was nothing actually to resent. Austin's invariable sweetness—his unbounded love for her—his trust in her, almost as implicit as a child's—she could not be angry with him.

"I am so sorry, my dear," said he penitently, "but I had no idea of the state of our finances. As Hal says—it is you who manage everything. I will ask him to take a smaller check—say just five pounds—when he comes back again."

"When he comes back again!" repeated Susannah bitterly. "He will not come back."

Nor did he. They waited dinner—half an hour—an hour—Austin was so certain that his brother had "turned over a new leaf"—except, perhaps, in punctuality at meals. They then sent down to the village in search of "the gentleman who had been at the rectory;" not saying "the rector's brother," lest he might be found at the public-house—though that was unlikely, drink not being one of Hal's besetting sins. But they found him nowhere. He had vanished—probably by some field-path, to the nearest railway station—with the check in his pocket, and nothing more was heard of him for years.

CHAPTER IV.

"Happy is the nation which has no history," and happy is the family without any startling incidents to break the smooth current of its uneventful years.

Such, for a long time, was the lot of the little family at the rectory—really a family now—father, mother, and child. And the child brought hope with it—hope and interest and joy in life. Sometimes Susannah, looking back upon old days, especially the dark days after her little baby died, wondered how she could have borne them.

She had an easier life now in many ways than she had ever known. Of money—alas! how the lack of it, or the wrong use of it, strikes at the very root of family peace!—of money there was enough, though nothing to spare, for with a larger income came heavier claims, as must always be the case with a clergyman. Still, the sharp struggle of poverty was over for ever with Austin and Susannah: and they soon grew to love dearly the pretty rectory, and simple country parish, which had been to them a refuge, though late, from the storms of life, and where they were content to lie at anchor for the rest of their days.

Of course, no human lives can be quite free from cares,

and they had theirs; but in most lives, if we investigate them, far fewer troubles come from without than from within: and the Trevenas had known enough of real sorrows never to invent for themselves imaginary or unnecessary ones. They were glad of happiness, and made the most of it whenever it came.

For days, weeks, months, Austin expected his brother's reappearance with a nervous anxiety—a mingled hope and fear that was trying enough to his wife. But Hal never did reappear, or make any sign of existence. Austin's hope, and Susannah's fear—a double fear now, since that truly "wicked" look which she had caught directed against her child—gradually subsided.

Also another unspoken dread, which when Arthur grew up from "the beautifullest baby that ever was seen," whom all the village was proud of, into a really splendid boy, began to dawn upon his adopted mother. What if his real mother should by and by crave after the treasure she had thrown away, and institute a search for him? Suppose she, or her emissaries, should find him, lie in wait for him, perhaps steal him—one or two stories of kidnapped children were in the newspapers just then, of which she read every line with a thrill of sympathetic anguish.

And once, when Manette and Arthur were missing for three hours, having contrived to lose themselves in a primrose wood, they came back, hungry and happy, laden with primroses, to find Mrs. Trevena white as death, sitting on a gravestone in the churchyard, having walked miles and miles in every direction in search of her child. She clasped him to her heart in such a passion of love and tears that Mr. Trevena, who came out for his evening stroll just in time to see the happy denouement of this temporary tragedy, was quite perplexed.

"My dear, it all comes from your vivid imagination. Don't sup sorrow with a long spoon. He is a dear child, I own that," and the rector patted kindly the curly head which nestled on his wife's shoulder. "But I don't think anybody is likely to steal him. Babies are as plentiful as blackberries, and you must remember, Susannah, that everybody does not consider him as valuable as you do."

She laughed, confessing she had been "very silly." But for weeks she scarcely let Arthur out of her sight; and Manette had strict orders never to go beyond the garden, the village, and the path leading to the great house, and on no account to answer any one she met who might question her about the boy.

This was literally the only event of the first six years of Arthur's life—the six happy infantine years, all pleasantness and play, with no lessons to learn, for he was not a precocious child, and his mother preferred physical to mental development. His education had begun indeed, as it can begin with every child, and should, even at six months old; but it was the unconscious education, imbibed daily and hourly from everything around him.

By and by, life became to little Arthur a perpetual question, which he always expected his mother to answer. She did answer, taking unwearied trouble to satisfy the opening mind and heart, never throwing the child back upon himself, or stifling his natural curiosity about the wonderful world he had come to. But sometimes she found herself fairly puzzled and obliged to own, frankly and humbly, "I don't know," upon which he once turned upon her with the grave answer, "But, mammy, you *ought* to know." A rebuke that made her study the question—something about a steam-engine—and tell him all about it next day.

Dr. Franklin's saying, when they were discussing the future of her baby, "I don't know whether you will educate him, but I am quite certain he will educate you," came back upon her often as an amusing truth. She knew herself to be a better woman, and certainly her husband was no worse man, nor a less happy man, for having that bit of continual sunshine, "a child in the house."

"I wish Dr. Franklin could see us," she often thought and said. But the worthy Kentuckian seemed to have melted away into thin air. For two or three years they got a letter from him, generally about the time of his godson's birthday, hoping the little fellow was quite well, and doing credit to his adopted family; but the letters were brief and formal; the doctor was a practical man and no great scribe. It scarcely surprised the Trevenas when, after a while, his letters ceased, and theirs gained no answer.

"Perhaps he is dead," Susannah thought, sadly, "and my boy has one friend less in the world."

Arthur had no lack of friends now, at any rate. He was a most popular little person. Everybody "spoiled" him; except that love never spoils. It is the alternation of harshness and weak indulgence which ruins many a poor, helpless child, who is made detestable to everybody, not through its own fault, but the fault of its relations.

With "King" Arthur it was not so. His mother's tender hand knew how to hold the reins firmly. Her yea was yea—her nay, nay; and the child soon found it out. His will—and he had a pretty strong one, poor little man!—was early taught that it must be used, not to govern others, but himself. Consequently, though impetuous, passionate, and full of boyish mischief and fun, he was neither a naughty nor a disagreeable child. From the "big" house, with its constantly changing tenants, down to every cottage in the parish, everybody made a pet of "King" Arthur.

So did his "papa," when the boy grew old enough to be interesting. Perhaps, under no circumstances would Mr. Trevena have been a model father; he was too self-absorbed, too much of the student, and it was by a curious natural instinct that Arthur always called him "papa," and Mrs. Trevena "mother." But he was very fond of the little fellow, who always amused and never troubled him, as ordinary papas are troubled by their offspring. And his kindness, his invariable sweet temper, and even his little oddities, attached the child to him almost as much as if he had been really his own. For to the young the "tie of blood" means nothing; and kindness, tenderness, the habit of propinquity, everything. A child often loves its nurse far better than its mother—an unheeding, unloving mother; and many parents and children, separated of necessity for years, have felt bitterly that with all their efforts it was absolutely impossible to reunite the broken bond.

But Arthur and his adopted parents lived so happily together, that everybody outside seemed to have forgotten he was not their own; and indeed they almost forgot it themselves, till something happened which startled Susannah into uneasy previsions. Long after it was past, she, like another holy mother, "pondered these things in her heart," and thanked God she had had strength to meet the difficulty; to face the first of many inevitable ills, and to face it in time.

Arthur came in to her, one day, with his poor little nose bleeding, and his whole frame quivering with passion and excitement. He had been playing in the garden with the gardener's boy, not a bad boy in his way; and at six years old Mrs. Trevena held class distinctions unnecessary; but there had evidently been some *fracas* between the children.

"My boy—how could Bob let you hurt yourself? He was the eldest; he ought to have taken care of you."

"He shall never take care of me again. I hate Bob! And I didn't hurt myself. We were fighting. But I've hurt him twice as much as he hurt me."

And the little fists were clenched, and the chest heaved with rage. The "devil" was roused in the heretofore "angel-boy,"—as from his sweet looks some of the villagers called him.

"You fought? Who began it?" said the mother gravely.

"I did. Bob told a lie, and I hit him. I'll hit him again to-morrow."

"Hush!" said Mrs. Trevena, but wisely abstained from any moral lectures till she had soothed her boy's physical sufferings; and he lay in her arms, pale and exhausted, angry but quiet, and quite "good," with that air of entire content which a child of his age finds nowhere if not on the mother's bosom.

"Now, my darling," she whispered, "tell me all about it."

But Arthur turned his head away, with the deep blush of sensitive childhood.

"I'd rather not tell you, please, mammy."

She would not compel him—it is right to respect even a babyish secret; but she urged tenderly, "Don't you think you would be happier if you told me?" And then it all came out.

"Bob said what was not true. He told me my papa was not my papa, and that my mammy, my own mammy, was not my mother." And hiding his face on her shoulder, Arthur once more burst into a passion of sobs.

Susannah felt as if an arrow had gone through her heart. Often and often had she considered this question, and decided that as soon as ever he could take it in, Arthur must be told the whole truth concerning himself. But the difficulty—the almost impossibility—of making so young a child comprehend any difference between adopted and real parenthood had caused her to defer this explanation from time to time, till some opportune moment should come. It had come. There was a brief pause of cowardly shrinking, and then she braced herself and seized the chance, which to let go by might be fatal. Perfect truthfulness, she had all along felt, would be the only safe as well as the only right course—for her darling's sake.

"My boy," she said, "I am sorry you fought—because what Bob said *was* true."

Arthur opened wide eyes of incredulous terror. "No—no! Mammy, I am your child—I am your child."

"Yes, my darling—my only darling! but not my born child—you are my adopted child."

"What does that mean?"

"My chosen child. Nobody cared for you or loved you—but mammy loved you, mammy chose you. Listen, and I'll tell my boy a little story."

It was the "quite true" story of her finding the bit of sweetwilliam, and how she planted it, and watered it, and watched it grow into a beautiful root, till she loved it better than any root in her garden.

"As mammy loves me," said the boy, brightening up and taking it all in, as he did any story, with delighted eagerness. "And mammy chose it—as she did me. Then I am mammy's own child after all."

"Always—always!" and she strained him to her heart—the unmistakable mother's heart, where he rested, satisfied. Childless mother—motherless child! Surely He who said to John, "Son, behold thy mother," and to Mary, "Mother, behold thy Son," often gives a special consecration to such relationships. It might be better for many a lonely household, many a forlorn child, if there were more of the like.

Determined not to let the golden moment pass by, but to seize this chance of making things clear, so that her boy might know all painful facts while so young that he should never remember the time when he had not known them, Susannah went on to explain how she and "papa" had found him among the mountains, brought him home to the rectory, and made him their son, as he would always be; that he must grow up a man—a good man, like papa—and take care of them both in their old age.

"And if Bob, or any one, ever tells you mammy does not love you as some mothers love their sons, say, she loves you more—because she chose you."

"As I chose my black kitten when the boys were going to drown it?"

"Yes! And would you like to hear why mammy called you Arthur?" continued she, wishing to drive out all pain from the infant mind, and perhaps impress it for life. "Shall I tell you another story?"

Mother's "'tories" were the unfailing panacea for every earthly ill. It is astonishing how much you can make a child understand if you only put it in words simple enough. Arthur already knew all about the wooden horse of Troy, Romulus and Remus, Queen Berengaria, and Richard Cœur de Lion, and even the story of several plays of Shakspere. Now, he listened with wide eyes fixed on that placid heaven, the mother's face; and sucking his two middle fingers—a trick he had when supremely happy—listened to the story of King Arthur; the "little naked child" who was found on the sea-coast of Cornwall, and brought up by Merlin. ("Was Merlin like my papa?" interjected Arthur)—how the baby grew to be a noble knight, a valiant soldier, and at last a king.

"Shall I ever be a king, mammy?" asked the small listener, with a look so radiant that his weak-minded mother thought he really might have been! Nevertheless she answered gravely:

"No, my boy, I am quite sure you never will be a king—except mammy's King Arthur. And something else too—a good, brave man. Brave men are never ashamed to own they are wrong: so we'll come and speak to Bob before he goes home, and say we both are sorry you fought with him, because you know now that he did not tell a lie. Come."

Arthur came. He did not speak to Bob, but his mother spoke for him, explaining that "my son"—as she carefully called him—now knew all about himself; that there must be no more references to the subject, and no more fighting. He was Master Arthur Trevena, and she should dismiss any servant who did not treat him as such.

Susannah said all this calmly—but a sharp inward pain was gnawing at her heart all the while, until she overheard Arthur's Parthian thrust at his discomfited foe.

"I won't fight you again, Bob—and I'll play with you to-morrow. I'm a deal better off than you—for your mother had to take you whether she liked you or not—my mother chose me!"

So off he marched—the little "King"—with a proud and gallant air; holding by his mother's hand, and entirely contented with his lot.

She was contented too; for now there was no more mystery—her boy would never have the pang of finding out suddenly that he was not her boy. Though with the sensitive reticence of childhood, he never referred to the matter again, never asked her a single question; but accepted with unlimited trust the love in which he lived as in perpetual sunshine. Only, night after night, as his mother sat down beside him, to tell him "just one little 'tory" before he went to sleep—the story he liked best, and asked for oftenest, was that of King Arthur.

So life went on at the rectory—a smooth, untroubled stream—

> "The constant stream of love which knew no fall,
> Ne'er roughened by those cataracts and breaks
> Which humor interposed too often makes."

Years afterwards, when reading that exquisite poem, Arthur recognized—as we do recognize when things are past—the picture of his happy childhood, and in Cowper's mother the portrait of his own.

Years slipped by—almost like a dream. From the baby he grew into the child—the boy—a big boy, though not yet a schoolboy—for there was no day-school near. Mrs. Trevena, who for many years had been a governess, taught him all she knew. By and by, Mr. Trevena, inquiring anxiously about his Latin and Greek —to the rector the one necessity of human learning— volunteered to continue both. So Arthur, who was neither a genius nor a dunce, but something between the two—a boy with plenty of brains, if he would only use them—gradually approached the time when life ceases to be all play, and it begins to dawn upon even the idlest boy, or the one most keen after physical enjoyments, that there is such a thing as work.

It did upon Arthur, though only occasionally. He was by no means a model boy. He honestly owned he "hated" his lessons, and only did them "to please mother," which secondary reason she perforce accepted, and made use of to his good. Doubtless she would have preferred a studious boy to an idle one; but then he was such a good boy, neither a prig nor a hypocrite; and sometimes when she saw his strong temptations—the exuberant youthful health and the joy in it—that pure joy of living which she herself had never known—she forgave him everything.

Perhaps both his adopted parents loved him all the better for being so unlike themselves—for bringing into their quiet household new elements which otherwise would have been unknown there; young companions, games, athletic sports. The Reverend Austin had never played cricket in his life; yet after going to see Arthur play, he was allured into lending one of his glebe-fields to the village cricket club; and would watch them with mild approval many a summer evening. And many a winter morning did Mrs. Trevena spend beside the large pond at Tawton Abbas—just to see Arthur skate. Though she felt sometimes like an old hen with one duckling—scarcely able to hide her terror at every tumble and every crack on the ice—still she did hide it, and gloried in her boy's height, agility, and grace. Above all in his perfect fearlessness, physical and moral.

Spite of his little faults—and he had his share—Arthur possessed one quality, the root of all good in either man or woman—he was not a coward. From infancy, the only fear he knew was the grave rebuke of his mother's face; generally a silent rebuke, for she rarely scolded and never whipped him; but her mute displeasure was more than he could stand. It brought him to his right mind at once—to the sobbing "I'll be good, mammy!" of infancy—to the half proud, half humble "I'm so sorry, mother," of boyhood. The turning away of her face from him was like the sun going out of the sky—he could not bear it. And once when he had to bear it, for two whole days—for his unconquerable idleness had so vexed her that she put the books away, and refused to open them again, his agony of distress made him actually ill. It was the turning-point; that contest between parent and child, which if the latter is allowed to win, is a defeat—to both—for life.

Susannah was a very gentle woman; but she could be stern, if need be, stern and hard as stone. When, after two, nay, three days of being sent to Coventry, and a fourth day, when he literally cried himself sick, Arthur came humbly, his books under his arm, and implored her to forgive him, she replied sadly:

"Forgiving is not forgetting. You have made mother's heart ache as it never ached before. Listen, my boy —for you are a boy now, not a baby." And she put her hand on his shoulder and looked searchingly into his face, as if longing to find there, what people cannot always find in their very own children, the qualities they themselves most value. "Arthur—for these twelve years papa and I have done our very best for you. We cannot do more. The rest you must do for yourself."

"How do you mean, mammy dear? Are you going to send me away—to school?"

G

"No—for we could not afford it. How could papa, with his small income, pay a hundred and fifty a year for your schooling—and you to be as idle then as you are now? It would not be right. I would not let him do it. No, if you want education you must get it for yourself—or go without it and grow up a dunce."

"And then you will wish you had left me to die at the roadside, instead of planting me like your sweetwilliam root. Perhaps you are right, mother."

Susannah started—she thought Arthur had long forgotten that little story; but one never knows what a child forgets or remembers.

There was a pause of pain—and then she said, "My son, I shall never wish things different from what they have been. And I am content with you just as you are, if you will only make the best of what you are. Do you think King Arthur would ever have been a soldier and a king, if he had not learnt his lessons?"

"Did he learn lessons? And—did he *like* them?" asked Arthur dolefully—so dolefully that Mrs. Trevena could not help laughing. At which the young sinner ventured to laugh too—kissed and hugged her, vehemently promising amendment. She shook her head—he had promised so often, and forgot it next day. How many "grown-ups" do the same! It sometimes struck Susannah as a curious fact that while all allowances are made for grown-up people, none are made for children. Though hard as the nether millstone in keeping Arthur in the right way—never for a moment pretending that wrong was right—she had great pity for his little aberrations; his laziness, his feather-headedness, and the like.

And when she looked at his broad brow and thoughtful eyes—inherited, heaven only knew from whom!—she took heart of grace that heaven would make all right in time.

One never knows when an arrow strikes home. "In the morning sow thy seed—in the evening withhold not thy hand." Such had been Susannah's principle all her days. She did her best; and then she rested in hope—which sometimes died—most often died!—but now and then it lived and blossomed—as now.

One day—after a week of most astonishing industry, Arthur said suddenly, "Mother, you told me I was to get education for myself. How am I to get it?"

She was not taken by surprise; for years she had pondered over the question—as she did everything that concerned her boy's future. She had said truly, that to send Arthur to a boarding-school was impossible. Even if possible, it would scarcely have been right. Her husband in his old age would need all his own money; he must not be stinted in anything for the sake of a son—who was not his son. Passionately as she loved her boy, Susannah held the balance of justice even. So she answered firmly:

"Arthur, if you are to grow up a clever man like papa you must do as he did;—you must get to be a Winchester boy—and then take yourself to New College, Oxford, with a Winchester scholarship. Mother would so like to see you in cap and gown!"

"Would you?" said he, with the sudden look which she loved to see—the bright, eager, purpose-like look—"Then, I'll try."

They went into the matter at once. Mr. Trevena,

who at the mention of Winchester pricked up his ears like an old war horse, needed little persuasion to take his wife and son to see his old haunts and revive his old acquaintanceships. One of the masters happened to be a schoolfellow of fifty years back; they fraternized joyfully, and wandered about together—Mrs. Trevena and Arthur following—through the chapel and courts, the schoolrooms and playgrounds, dear to all Wykehamites, where generation after generation of boys have worked and played and passed away. Here and there were mementoes of some of them who had made themselves famous in after-life, and of others—Arthur's eye brightened, and his mother's heart trembled, as they stood looking at them—who had died early, mostly on the field of battle, only a year or two after being Winchester boys.

Susannah was an ambitious woman—what mother of a son would not be? When Arthur whispered to her, "I mean to be a Winchester boy," she pressed his arm in silence as they walked together—he very proud of being fully as tall as she. They understood one another, and were happy.

This was the bright side of things; but there was another side, of which she had had prevision, but never so clearly as to-day.

The master stood explaining to her various things—while Mr. Trevena went to show Arthur the picture of the Faithful Servant. She learnt that a certificate of baptism must be sent in, to prove the boy's age—over twelve and under thirteen—and that the examination, in which there were often nearly a hundred candidates for fourteen scholarships, was about the middle of July.

'My son will be thirteen next June," said Susannah —who always took care to say " my son " to strangers.

" Then he has only one chance. He will have to work hard for it—but no doubt he will. He is "—glancing carelessly at Arthur, who stood a few yards off, and making the superficial remark that so many think proper —" he is so very like his father."

Whether the boy overheard, she could not tell—if he had, no doubt he would, in his simplicity, only have thought it " funny " that he should resemble his gray, stooping, elderly papa; but Susannah felt herself grow hot all over. She could not answer—any explanation at that moment was impossible—yet she felt like a deceiver—acting inevitably, righteously, but yet a deceiver. And how would her boy feel? not now perhaps—he was too young to take it in—but by and by?

" I ought to explain——," she began, with a desperate firmness. At that moment Mr. Trevena and Arthur came up, rendering explanation impossible. The train was nearly due : they were late—as the good rector had a trick of being—only a minute remained for polite adieux, and they hurried away.

But as Susannah sat silent, watching the landscape whirl past, in that noisy peace which allows such time for thinking—a new anxiety awoke in her heart.

She had resolved to send her boy to school, for she felt he must go; his nature required the spur of emulation to learn well; but she had not taken in all that this involved. Her neighbors, the simple folk of Tawton Magna, had long since accepted the truth, and then forgot—as the Trevenas had almost forgotten themselves—

that Arthur was not their own child. Not a word to the contrary was now ever said to him or them. But in the wider world to which Arthur was going, and must go, things were sure to be said—cruel things, perhaps—from which his mother could no longer protect him.

Had he been a girl, it would have been different. She could then have kept her child beside her; no need to go to school at all; or to pass from the shelter of the mother's wing, except into some honorable happy home, where she was loved for herself—married for herself. Many a King Cophetua lives to bless the day he wooed his "beggar-maid," and especially, if she has no blood relations! But a boy must face the world—stand on his own feet—fight his own battles. What if Arthur's school-fellows came to find out his history? how they might torment him!—there is nothing crueller than your ordinary schoolboy. How lads with real fathers and mothers might jeer at "Nobody's child"!

Susannah clenched her hands under her shawl. She felt she should like to do something—to hurt somebody, who dared to hurt her child. The "wild animal" feeling, which makes the tamest creatures dangerous when their young are attacked, came into her, till she almost laughed at herself, and then could have cried at her own helplessness. Yet tears were idle. The thing was inevitable—he must bear it. How could she help him to bear it?

"Tell the truth and shame the devil" was, as ever, the only chance for her boy; and after all, he was a boy —"with hands to war and fingers to fight"—as old King David had, and blessed the Lord for. Alas! in this our world they are only too necessary! Arthur had moral courage too, as had been lately proved when a neighboring curate, hearing the boy's voice in church, offered to teach him singing, and music too; and, in spite of his companions, the young millionaires at Tawton Abbas, calling it "girlish," he persisted in steadily strumming on the rectory piano, and never missing an hour of the village choir practice. Music, in fact, was the only thing he really worked at, with all his heart in it. Once his mother—listening to the lovely boy-voice, and hearing from the ritualistic curate, Mr. Hardy, what a remarkable talent he had in that direction—recalled, almost with a pang, the story of that opera-singer who had run away from Milan—who might have crossed the St. Gothard, and stopped at Andermatt—who might have been—— But speculations were idle—worse than idle—dangerous. She shut up all these things in her heart, seeing that, however it came, her boy's talent for music was there, and irrepressible. Nor did she try to repress it; she only insisted that he should work, not idle at it: and do his other work steadily, meantime.

He did. Mr. Hardy, the musical curate, who, like many more, combined music and mathematics, offered to help him in his Euclid and algebra; the rector taught him Latin and Greek; his mother, and the faithful Manette, now promoted from nurse to cook, and likely to be a fixture at the rectory, helped him in his French. So all was in train for the Winchester examination, to which he must go up, in July—a big boy of thirteen— for those three anxious days which would probably decide his lot for life.

As the time approached, Mrs. Trevena, spite of her smooth brow and quiet smile, would thankfully "have given worlds"—as the phrase is—not to put it off—it was her way always to face things—but to know that it was safe over.

Another thing which she had to face she did put off, unintentionally, till the very last day. Then having settled everything, and even packed her boy's box and her own—they were to stay together with Mr. Trevena's old school-fellow during the three days of examination—she and Arthur walked up and down together along their favorite walk, the peach-tree walk, under a high south wall. Susannah was now growing old enough to love the shelter of a south wall and the smooth ease of a gravel walk. But age had no terrors, for was not her boy's strong arm round her waist, and his bright face beside her? In his young life she lived anew, perhaps even a happier life than her own.

"If you are tired, mammy, let us sit down." Arthur always saw when his mother was tired, quicker even than her husband did; but then he was such a practical boy, and not a bit of a bookworm. "You stop here in the summer-house, and I'll help Bob Bates to gather the peas for dinner."

"No, not yet," for she had something to say which must be said before he went to Winchester, only it was difficult to begin. "Bob is a big boy now, almost as tall as his father."

"Bob is ever so much older than I am," said Arthur, a little aggrieved. "I'll be as tall as my papa some day."

"I hope so, dear." Then, suddenly facing the evil,

though it made her heart beat almost with the pulsations of her youth, "Does Bob Bates ever speak to you now about what you fought over, years ago?"

"What was that, mammy? I forget.—No," with a quick blush, the sensitive blush so ready to come and go on his fair face. "No, I think I remember. It was about my not being papa's own boy, and yours. No, nobody ever says a word to me now."

"That is well."

They walked on in silence, she thinking how best to put the next thing she had to say, when he saved her the saying of it.

"Mother, if anybody speaks to me like that at Winchester, what am I to do? Shall I fight them?"

She paused a minute. It was so hard, so hard!

"No, my dear. I see no good in fighting. Nobody means you any harm, and nothing they say can alter anything. It is the truth. No brave man need be afraid of the truth. I am sure King Arthur never was."

"Did anybody ever say to him—what Bob Bates used to say to me?"

"Very likely, for his parentage was never known. But he was such a noble knight in himself that nobody ever cared to ask where he sprang from. It will be the same with you, if you grow up a good man."

"But I shall never be a king, and have Knights of the Round Table."

"I am afraid not. What would you like to be?"

Now the great event in the boy's life was his having been lately taken by his friend the High Church curate to Exeter, where he heard an oratorio and an opera. It should not have been a pang, and yet it was—when he answered with enthusiasm, "I should like to be an opera singer!" his mother started as if she had been shot.

But she answered calmly, "Well, my son, boys often make resolves, and break them. I knew one little fellow who was determined to be Lord Chancellor, but he changed his mind and said he would be an omnibus-driver. However, just now, you can only be one thing —a Winchester boy. Try for that."

"I will," said Arthur firmly, "because I know mother would like it."

"Thank you," pressing the arm that was round her waist. Youths often like to make love to a little mother, no bigger than themselves. She looked at him, the boy that any mother might be proud of—that any childless mother might have craved after with frantic longing— and that his own mother had thrown away. No matter! he was *her* son now—hers, Susannah's—by every right of justice and duty, if not nature; and no power on earth should ever snatch him from her.

She was not sorry to have to take him to Winchester herself, and make friends for him there, whether he succeeded or failed; she had begun to feel that their shut-up life would never do for a growing boy. He would need companions; and their only near neighbors, except the villagers, were the tenants of Tawton Abbas; families continually changing, for the idiot heir of the Damerels still lived on, and it was said that when he died there would be a grand fight between two distant cousins for the title and estate. Meanwhile, the lovely old house was sometimes let, sometimes stood empty, and the rectory family had the run of the park and gardens. But of society they had almost none. This did not matter to Austin and Susannah, but it did to Arthur, who, now risen above the level of Bob Bates, often wished for "somebody to play with—somebody young." And therefore, though parting with him would be like cutting off her right hand, his mother had determined to send him to school.

"Mr. Hardy and papa both say you can pass if you try. You must try. Think how grand it would be to have your name on the Roll."

"And to go and live at Winchester, where I can hear the cathedral service every day if I like, and learn to sing in the college chapel."

"You could learn anything, my boy, if you would only give your mind to it—you idle monkey. But you will work now? You'll do your very best, and if you fail—well—we'll try something else—

'But screw your courage to the sticking place,
And we'll not fail!'"

"Bravo, mother! You are such a brick! You ought to be a boy yourself."

They laughed, thoroughly understanding one another. Then not sorry for a brief pause of solitude, in the nervous strain which was greater than she knew, she sent Arthur off for a walk across the park, and sat down under the acacia tree on the rectory lawn, watching idly the swallows flying over the glebe-meadows, where the cows were feeding, and the trees stood motionless in the summer silence of the newly-shorn, fresh, green fields.

A peaceful, lovely picture! grown each year more familiar and more dear. Susannah hoped to watch it year after year until she died. For she felt sure her husband would never leave Tawton Magna. He was not ambitious—had no desire of church promotion. He too was quite content with his life. Her eyes followed him, sauntering up and down the peach-tree walk, writing in his head his next Sunday's sermon. She thought of all his goodness, gentleness, and tenderness, not only to her but to her boy; and it seemed as if no woman ever had a happier life than she—a life to which no change could ever come.

At that minute—it is strange how often these coincidences happen—Arthur came running to her with a letter.

"A boy brought it. I met him at the gate. He says he has to wait for an answer."

"Take it to papa," she was just saying carelessly, when something struck her as familiar in the handwriting—terribly familiar. Many people know what it is—the heart-sinking at sight of one particular handwriting, which has been the curse of the family for a lifetime.

"Mother, you look so white! What is the matter?"

"Nothing, dear boy. I will take papa his letter."

It was from Hal Trevena. He was in a small public-house of the neighboring town, with his wife and child, and without a halfpenny.

So he said, at least, adding that the inconvenience was but temporary, as they were on their way to "some wealthy friends of Mrs. Trevena's residing in Wales."

Only the said Mrs. Trevena had broken down on the way, and lay dangerously ill, which was, the husband added, "most inconvenient." He begged for "a small loan," and that his brother would go and see him.

"Poor Hal—poor Hal—of course I must go," said the rector, with a deprecating, distressed look. "And you would not object—to my giving him a little money?"

"No, of course not." She took her husband's hand, and sat down on the bench beside him, in a sort of dull submission to fate. The roses were blooming, the bees humming in them, over the pretty summer-house: the swallows were darting across the high blue sky, and the cows feeding in the meadow, just as they had done ten minutes ago, when she had felt so happy, so thankful to God for her happiness. And now——

"Poor Hal," repeated Austin uneasily. "A sick wife, does he say? and he never was used to illness, any more than I. But I suppose I ought to go to them."

Susannah thought a minute, then she said, "Shall I go instead of you?"

"Oh, if you would! My dear, how kind of you!"

Mrs. Trevena never answered. She knew it was not kindness at all, only a desperate preventive against danger which she foresaw, and could meet, but Austin could not.

"So very kind," he repeated. "But you forget—you were to take the boy to Winchester to-morrow."

"Mr. Hardy would take him instead of me. And he might perhaps be as well alone. He must learn to face the world some time," she added, with a sad kind of smile. "At any rate, I will go now, and come back as soon as I can."

But she did not come back. It was only a half-hour's walk, yet Arthur and his papa sat expecting her in vain, hour after hour—till—almost for the first time in his life—the boy had to go to bed without his mother's good-night kiss. Late, almost at midnight, a messenger arrived, bringing two letters; one to Arthur—the first he had ever received—explaining that he must go to Winchester "like a man" with Mr. Hardy, and do his very best, so that whether he succeeded or failed in getting the scholarship, his mother might be proud of her boy.

To her husband she wrote even more briefly. "Hal's wife is dying. Her little girl—it was a girl, not a boy—is her only nurse. We must take them in. Tell Manette to get ready the spare room, and as soon as Arthur and Mr. Hardy are gone, send a fly here. There is little luggage—he has spent everything they had in the world. She will be better dead, poor soul!—but she ought to die peacefully in our house."

This was all Susannah wrote—or said.

Next day, in the dusk of the evening, her husband watched her superintend the carrying up-stairs of what seemed little more than a bundle of clothes, with a white ghastly face appearing out of it—that dying face which, it was plain to see, would never come down-stairs any more. Closely following came a little girl; a small elfish creature, with thin, starved, withered features, and great dark eyes—she seemed all eyes—watching the sick mother with a kind of fierce jealousy, as if to protect her from everybody else.

The husband and father did not appear.

"He will be here at supper-time—did he not say so, Nanny?" observed Mrs. Trevena, taking the child's hand.

"He said so—but we never believe what papa says," was the answer—with the cruel candor of ten years old.

So, there they were under her roof—Hal Trevena and his family. And her own boy's room was empty; and throughout the house was that terrible silence which marks the absence of a child—a noisy, merry, happy child.

She had done her duty—the duty which lay to her hand, so plain that she could not choose but do it; yet, as she laid her head down for the few minutes of sleep that she was able to snatch on the sofa, in the chamber of the dying woman, Susannah's pillow was wet with her tears.

CHAPTER V.

THE next two days went by in quiet—hopeless, passionless quiet. Life yet lingered in Halbert Trevena's wife; but they all knew—and she knew too, they thought—that nothing could save her. She was in the last stage of consumption, or rather atrophy; brought on, no doubt, by misery and privation. By making dives and guesses at truth through a mass of superincumbent fiction, Susannah gained from her brother-in-law something of the family history.

It appeared that Nanny—christened Anastasia—was their only child; the "son and heir," though not quite non-existent, having died soon after his birth. The millionaire father-in-law was also a creation of Captain Trevena's imagination; or, at any rate, whatever money the old man possessed had speedily been drained from him by his aristocratic son-in-law. During his lifetime he had protected his daughter and grandchild as well as he could; when he died both fell helplessly into the hands of that personage, to whom, unless he altogether outrages morality, the law persists in giving the rights—though he fulfills none of the duties—of "husband and father." The wife, a feeble creature, born to suffer and complain, had clung to him, probably because she had nothing else to cling to; and so they had drifted on, sinking or swimming, heaven knew how, or how long—it was useless to inquire—till they came to England and to Tawton Magna.

"Not that we meant to inflict ourselves upon you, except for a short visit," said Captain Trevena, with great dignity. "We thought of wintering at Bath—we were on our way thither when my dear invalid broke down. But I hope she will be better soon."

"She will be better soon," repeated Susannah; but he either could not or would not understand her meaning, and it was no use to press the fact; or the other one, that Tawton was not on the road to Bath at all. But fact and fiction were inextricably mingled in Captain Trevena's conversation. Susannah's only desire was to keep him out of his wife's sick-room—which was not difficult—he so hated illness; and let her slip quietly into that peace of death which was far better than life.

Poor woman!—what sort of woman she was or had been, mattered little now. Her sister-in-law inquired nothing. She did carefully all that could be done for "the remarkably fine woman"—who never could have been anything but a plain and rather common-looking person; she held with her firm soft clasp the dying hand —evidently not a lady's hand—and so thin that once in washing it, the wedding-ring slipped off.

"Don't put it on again—keep it for Nanny," was all the sick woman said; as if relieved at dying without that badge of slavery.

She never asked for her husband, but only for Nanny. And the child, who had none of the looks and ways of

H

childhood, scarcely ever left her bedside. Nanny was small, dark, and plain; exceedingly like her mother; "not a bit of a Trevena"—her father said, apologetically. He evidently did not care for her. Nor, candidly speaking, did Susannah herself feel much drawn to the little girl, except for her entire devotion to her poor mother.

During the long night-watches—for, feeling sure the end was near, she had never taken her clothes off since that sunny hour of ignorant peace under the acacia tree—the other mother sat and thought; looking anxiously ahead —as, possibly because Austin never did it, she was prone to do: weighing well the case, and considering every claim of duty, and of that much-belauded quality, self-sacrifice, which so seldom involves the sacrifice of only one's self. It did not here. To take Nanny as a permanent inmate—which seemed the most natural and right thing—would alter life entirely to the happy little family at the rectory. True, Arthur might go to school, and Nanny come in his place; but could Susannah love any child but Arthur? Certainly not Halbert Trevena's child. And to have him, the father, coming and going, tormenting Austin, perhaps sowing discord between him and her—or him and Arthur—it would be more than she could bear.

"But perhaps," she said to herself, "I may not have to bear it. He may want his daughter himself—or," she was almost ashamed of the thought—yet it was true —"the house which held his daughter would be the last place where he would care to go to."

She was in a great strait; dreading continually that

the dying woman should speak, and perhaps exact some death-bed promise that might burden her whole future—yet what could she do?

On the forenoon of the second day, seeing no change, she snatched half an hour of fresh air in the peach-tree walk—" mother's thinking-place," Arthur called it. There had been a letter from Arthur—telling how he had not as yet been " weeded out," as the incompetent boys were, day by day—a hopeful sign; but the tug of war was yet to come.

" And he is all alone by himself—my darling boy!" she thought, with the natural mother's pang and mother's yearning; then remembered that other mother who was about to leave her child " all alone by itself"—nay—worse than alone—for ever.

The soft sleepy summer day seemed quite dreadful in its calm. And she could speak to no one—least of all to her husband, who looked so worried and weary, who tried to smile, while his brother smoked in his study and drank his wine, and conversed with him from morning till night; loud talk—boasting talk, in which it was a severe brain-exercise to distinguish what was truth and what were—in plain English—lies.

Doubtless he was at it now—for she could smell a cigar in the summer-house; but the second voice there was not the rector's—it was the low whimpering of a child.

She had meant to avoid the spot; but now she walked right towards it. Susannah had one great weakness—she never could hear a child cry without going to see what was amiss.

There stood Captain Trevena, with his little girl before him. He held her by the shoulders and was shaking her as a big dog shakes a hare. And not unlike a hunted hare's was the look of those frightened pathetic eyes.

"I'll teach you to hide things from your father," he was saying—in a voice very different from his bland conversation-tone. "Wait till your mother is dead—and then—— Once more—where does she keep that diamond ring?"

"Mother made me promise not to tell anybody—and I won't tell," sobbed the child.

"You won't? Then, take that—and that—and that."

With each word came a blow—what the advocates of corporal punishment for children would call "just a box on the ear." But blows they were; and they rang loudly on either side of the poor little head—the head with the delicate brain.

Susannah darted forward—"Brute!" she muttered beneath her breath: and snatched Nanny out of reach of the father's hand—the hand—nominally that of a man and a gentleman—lifted against a child. Taking the little girl in her arms—though ten years old Nanny was piteously small and light—Mrs. Trevena faced her brother-in-law with flashing eyes.

Brutes are almost always cowards. Captain Trevena's rage evaporated in the mildest politeness.

"I am sorry you should have come at such an inopportune moment. A little wholesome chastisement—all parents must have the pain of administering it sometimes. But perhaps your boy is so perfect that he never requires whipping?"

"I should scorn to whip him. I should feel that every blow I gave to him was a degradation to myself. And for your child—touch her again if you dare!"

Then the superficial gloss melted off, and the "brute" nature—harsh word, but true!—re-asserted itself.

"You had better not interfere between me and Nanny. I'll do as I like with my own."

"You will not," said Susannah resolutely. "No man's child is his own to do as he likes with. He must be a true parent or he has no parental rights at all. Nanny! little Nanny!"

But the child heard nothing. She had fainted.

"You see?" said Susannah, showing the white little face which lay on her shoulder. "Now go. It is the best thing you can do."

She said not another word—her scorn was too great. Under it he slunk away to the other end of the garden: where half an hour afterwards, when Nanny was quite recovered, having made no word of complaint or explanation except "Don't tell mother," he was seen walking and smoking with leisurely grace, just as if nothing had happened.

From that moment Mrs. Trevena's mind was made up. She did not feel particularly drawn to Nanny, who was not an interesting child; but she was a child, and every womanly and motherly feeling in Susannah's nature revolted from the thought of her being left helpless, motherless, in the hands of such a father.

"I don't want to do it—I would prefer not to do it," she said to her husband in the few minutes' talk they had together that night. "But there is no alternative. When Nanny's mother dies we must take the child."

"I suppose we must," said Austin with a troubled air. "But she is not the least bit of a Trevena."

"No, thank God!" Susannah was on the point of saying, but stopped, and leaning down kissed the wrinkled brow that she had loved ever since it was smooth and young. "You are the best man I ever knew in all my life. You do your duty whatever comes. Do it still, Austin, and—so shall I."

Before settling again to her nightly watch, she tucked up little Nanny in her sofa-bed, and kissed her—kindly, rather than tenderly. She felt kindly to every child, but she had no heart of love for any but Arthur. Then seeing Nanny's mother was watching her—apparently wide awake, and wishing to talk—she came and sat down by the bedside, prepared for whatever might happen.

"Nanny is fast asleep—she was rather tired. She is a good little girl."

The gentle whisper was answered by a faint pressure of Susannah's hand. "Yes—very good. I want to speak to you—about Nanny."

It was not an hour for disguising, or delaying, the truth. Still, Mrs. Trevena could not help saying, "By and by, when you are better."

"I shall never be better. I don't want to be better—I want to die—except for Nanny." And as she spoke, very feebly and faintly, two great tears stole from the dying eyes, and rolled down the wasted cheeks.

All the mother in Susannah's heart yearned over this

other mother, obliged to go and leave her child alone in a cruel world. She paused a minute, and then said, though feeling keenly all that the promise involved, and how hard a sacrifice it was to make it, "Be content about Nanny. We—my husband and I—will always take care of her."

To her astonishment, the sick woman, instead of showing gratitude, fell into an agony of distress.

"No—no—no. It is the last thing I should wish. Let her be taken right away—brought up anyhow, anywhere —but not with the Trevenas. No Trevenas — no Trevenas," she kept muttering; while shudder after shudder passed over her.

Mrs. Trevena felt neither anger nor pain—not even surprise. In her sister-in-law's place she knew she should have said the same. There have been mothers—she could understand it—who would rather see their children die than leave them in the hands of their father.

"I am not a Trevena," she said soothingly. "Can you not trust me?"

The dying eyes opened; and the two women—both mothers—looked fixedly at each other. What different faces!—what different lives! But was it entirely Fate that had done it? Do we not constantly see some women who conquer Fate, and make peace out of misery? while others throw away the happiest lot and convert it into woe? However, this is a mystery which none can unravel: Susannah never attempted to do so.

She took her sister-in-law's hand, and by degrees succeeded in winning from her enough confidence to get some light on the dark future.

G

It seemed, the woman's one hope in coming to England had been that she might live long enough to place her child with her own former governess—a Miss Grogan—who kept a small school at Bath, and would educate Nanny, whether paid or not paid, until she could earn her own living; and also protect her from the one person in the world against whom she required protection—her father.

"Miss Grogan knows everything; she was with us in Australia—she is altogether faithful. Take Nanny to her—take her yourself, and don't tell him the address—Nanny knows it—only Nanny. Hide the child from him—hide her! If I could only hide her with me in the grave! she would be safe there."

"She shall be safe—I will see to that. Be satisfied."

Susannah's low firm voice and reassuring clasp, seemed to bring some comfort to the miserable woman, whose misery would soon be past. For such as she there is no refuge except death; and her sister-in-law knew it.

"Yes, I think I may trust you—as you said, you are not a Trevena. Look here!"

Opening her night-dress, she showed, suspended round her neck, a valuable ring. In the dim candlelight the stone—one huge diamond—glittered with a ghastly brightness on the poor withered breast, little more than skin and bone.

"When I am dead, take care of this. My father found it at Ballarat, and left it to Nanny. It is all she has. Don't let *him* see it—don't let him get it. You promise?"

"I promise."

And for the first time Susannah kissed her sister-in-law. When her lips touched the brow she felt the death-damp already gathering there. A violent fit of coughing came on, and after that there was quiet.

Should she disturb this last hour of peace? Susannah decided not. Should she call the household—or fetch the husband who was such only in name, and in reality a torment and a terror, to trouble the dying woman? The poor soul wished for nobody, asked for nobody; except that towards dawn, when there was a faint twitter of sparrows under the eaves outside, she opened her eyes and looked wistfully round.

"Where's Nanny?"

"Asleep on her sofa there; but I can lift her and put her beside you."

"Please, yes. Thank you. God bless you." Many a year after Susannah remembered that benediction.

She lifted the little girl, who half waked up, and then with a contented murmur put her arm round her mother's neck, and went to sleep again. Susannah would have moved it—the little soft arm, heavy with sleep—but the mother refused.

"No—no. Don't disturb the child."

They were her last words.

Mrs. Trevena had watched by many a death-bed, but this one was so peaceful that she hardly recognized it was such. Mother and child dropped asleep together so quietly and naturally that she thought the end might not come for a good while yet. She sat, watching the daybreak grow, little by little, full of many and anxious thoughts, that wandered far away into the dim future, making her forget the present. At last, hearing the church clock strike five, she rose softly to undraw the curtain, and returning to the bed, looked at the sleepers.

He had come—the great Divider. The child was breathing softly, in the deepest, happiest slumber; the mother—yes! she slept too: she would never wake to sorrow any more.

Susannah lifted Nanny in her arms, covering her face with a shawl: and carried her, still fast asleep, into the next room, where she laid her down in Arthur's bed. Then she came back; closed the eyes and straightened the limbs of the dead; and kneeling by the bedside wept, as she never thought she should have wept for Halbert Trevena's wife; scarcely with grief—but with a tenderness, the memory of which never departed from her heart.

When Captain Trevena descended to his usual late and solitary breakfast, he received the news of his wife's death, which he took so easily as quite to relieve Mrs. Trevena's conscience for not having summoned him before.

"Poor dear girl! Well—it was to be expected. I hope she did not suffer at the last?"

But whether or not she had suffered, or how and when she died, he did not stay to hear. His brother was a great deal more moved than he. Still, neither of them asked to enter the room, where, sweeter far in death than in life, the dead wife and mother lay.

It was not till nearly mid-day that Mrs. Trevena, who had left Nanny still sound asleep in Arthur's bed, heard through the silent house a wild cry, and found the child standing, half-dressed as she was, battering frantically against the locked door, and screaming aloud for "Mother!"

How Susannah got through the next half-hour, she hardly knew; how she managed to tell the child the truth, and gradually to quiet her despair. But in such crises words often come which seem like inspirations; and there was in Susannah's very silence—in the touch of her hand and her kiss, something so essentially motherly, that the motherless child at last sobbed herself to sleep on her bosom, and was again laid in Arthur's bed.

Then Mrs. Trevena went to her own; and overcome with sheer exhaustion, she too fell asleep.

When she woke up—tight, rough, boyish arms were round her neck, and she was almost smothered in kisses.

"Mammy, mammy. I've come back, and I'm on the Roll—fifth on the Roll. I've beaten ninety boys, though I never went to school. Next term I shall be a Winchester boy—and in five years more an Oxford man—for I'll try to get to New College. I *will*, mother! How glad you'll be!"

And Arthur was very much astonished to find his mother weeping on his neck as he had never seen her weep in all his life before. His had been such a happy young life; so entirely free from the shadow of death—from every shadow of every kind—that no wonder he was startled.

He had rushed in with his joyful news, to find the house empty and silent; for the two brothers were in the churchyard choosing a grave; and the servants were all in the kitchen "talking things over." No one had seen him arrive, or told him anything.

"I ran into the dining-room, and the parlor, and then up to my room—there's a queer little girl fast asleep in my bed—and then I ran in here. Mother, what is the matter? Why do you cry? Who has been vexing you?"

Mrs. Trevena made her son sit down by her—happy living child and living mother!—and explained all that had happened.

Some men, and boys too, have that best characteristic of true manhood—tenderness over the weak and the suffering. Mrs. Trevena had seen it in Arthur before now, but never so plainly as when he went with her—of his own accord—"to comfort poor little Nanny."

Nanny was awake, crying quietly, but not troubling anybody; it seemed to have been the law of her young life that she was not to trouble anybody.

"I have brought my son to see you, Nanny. Kiss her, Arthur." And the two children, with the wonderful freemasonry of childhood, kissed one another, and made friends immediately.

They were a great contrast; one so big and tall and strong; handsome too—bright-looking as bright-hearted; the other puny, dark, and plain—nothing at all attractive about her except large pitiful brown eyes, as pathetic as a hunted deer's. She looked up in the big boy's face, as if wondering if he too were going to hurt her—and then she began to smile.

Arthur took hold of the child's hand—he evidently thought her the merest baby; and proposed that she should go with him to see his big Newfoundland, Nero, and his pretty pigeons. And Nanny went.

Thankfully Mrs. Trevena saw that Arthur comforted the poor little girl twenty times better than she could have done. And it gladdened her to notice that during the next dreary three days he did not forsake the shut-up house, or get weary of the heartbroken and often fretful child. That deep pity which is always deepest in the strongest hearts, had been awakened in the boy. He was chivalrous, tender, and patient too, with poor Nanny, to a degree that his mother had hardly thought possible in a lively active lad of thirteen. But she rejoiced—as she did in every new development of character which foretold what sort of man her "King" Arthur would become.

He seemed to have quite forgotten his own success, which Mr. Hardy said had been most remarkable. Not a word was spoken about Winchester until the days of busy quiet "with death in the house" were ended, and Nanny's mother had been laid to rest in the churchyard close by.

Nanny was not at the funeral—nor Arthur. Mrs. Trevena sent the children away for a long walk across country, and when they came back the blinds were all drawn up and the house looking as usual. So Nanny's last remembrance of her mother was—as Mrs. Trevena had determined it should be—that peaceful falling asleep with her arm round her neck, as seemed to have been the habit of years.

Captain Trevena followed his wife to the grave with due decorum, and in a new suit of best black clothes, provided by his brother. Outsiders might have thought he mourned sincerely the wife whose life he had made utterly miserable. Perhaps he did regret her—for a day.

All that evening he was rather subdued and grave; spoke kindly to his daughter, and approved of her mourning-dress—arranged like everything else, by her "kindest of aunts"—to whom he left every responsibility. Except a passing remark about "a little ring—a sort of crystal, of no particular value,"—which, if she found, he should like to have, "to wear in remembrance of my late dear wife"—except this observation, which Mrs. Trevena never answered, he asked no question about anything. In truth there was nothing to inquire about. Save the clothes they had on, mother and child seemed to have possessed scarcely a rag in the world.

Captain Trevena was better off. And when at supper-time he announced that he should want Bob Bates to carry his portmanteau to the nearest station, as he thought of going to London—"for a few days' rest and change"—nobody attempted to hinder him.

He went, and it was a relief when he was gone. To see Nanny, whom he had forgotten to say good-bye to, break into a broad smile of happiness when told her father had departed, was the most piteous condemnation that any father could have earned.

"Mother, I hate that man! He is no more like my papa than—than——" words failed to Arthur's youthful indignation. "I'll never call him 'Uncle' as long as I live."

"You need not," answered the mother, gravely. "He is not your uncle, and Nanny is not your cousin; but you can always call her so."

"I will!—and I'll protect her to the end of my days." And Arthur looked as if he knew how much she needed protection—which, very likely, he did know, though with the not uncommon reticence of childhood the two young creatures kept their own counsel. It had been one of the chivalrous teachings of "King" Arthur's mother to her boy—"Never complain!"

No one was much surprised, or very sorry, when a whole week passed, and Captain Trevena did not reappear. Meantime, Mrs. Trevena, who never let grass grow under her feet when there was anything to be done, had written to the address which Nanny gave her —the child was a curious mixture of babyishness and sad precocity—and had received a neatly written and kindly worded letter, signed "Anastasia Grogan," saying the writer would be glad to receive her goddaughter immediately, in her quiet home at Bath.

"I will take Nanny there myself," said Susannah, explaining to her husband the dead mother's wish, and obeying it by not even telling him Miss Grogan's address: Austin was too tender-hearted to be trusted with a secret that concerned his clever brother. "And I think I will take her at once."

For she felt that with the then existing English law, which even yet maintains the fiction of mediæval and ancient days, that a man's wife and children are his mere goods and chattels to deal with as he chooses, it would not be safe to wait Captain Trevena's return.

Susannah was not a coward. She was determined, by fair means or foul, to snatch this poor innocent—a girl too—out of her father's hands; to circumvent him, and the law too, if necessary, by all possible means. She had no conscience-stings — no scruple about parental rights—there can be no rights where duties are left unfulfilled.

"God gave me no children," she sighed to herself, as she watched Arthur and Nanny at play in the garden—Nanny had blossomed out like a flower in that one week's peace and love. "But I have saved one child: perhaps it may be His will that I shall help to save another."

So, one fine morning—leaving a line for Austin, who had gone to a diocesan meeting—she started with the two, for she dared not leave Arthur behind, and, besides, he was company for Nanny. Her heart melted as she wrote the brief note, almost the first since her marriage, to her "beloved husband," from whom she had never been parted for a day. She knew her departure would vex and grieve him, but he would be glad afterwards. For sometimes, in the relief and peace of his brother's absence, the rector had begun to notice his little niece, and once had even taken her on his knee, and remarked that she had "the Trevena hands."

"She is, after all, the last of the Trevenas—his own flesh and blood: if I can save her, Austin will be glad."

So thought the faithful wife—faithful, though stern—as the train whirled her away to Bath, she sitting silent, and her two "children" opposite chattering like a couple of magpies. Two children—neither of them her own, yet God seemed to have given them to her, and she accepted the trust. If she could only make them His children, her life would not have been in vain.

Had Miss Grogan proved unsatisfactory, she had determined, at all risk and cost, to bring Nanny back to the rectory; but it was needless. She found a bright little house, on the top of one of the pleasant Bath hills, and in it a bright little woman—Irish, certainly, but of that type of Irishwoman which English folk are so slow to believe in. Tidy, accurate, methodical; keeping her house "in apple-pie order," and herself "as neat as a new pin;" to these proverbially un-Irish qualities Miss Grogan added others, which even enemies allow to the children of the Emerald Isle—a warm heart, a blithe spirit, quick sympathy, and ready generosity. Withal, that most desirable thing in man or woman—courage. Elderly as she was, there was a sparkle in Miss Grogan's soft Irish eyes which showed that she knew how to defend a friend and to face a foe. Susannah felt instinctively that the poor feeble dead woman had judged rightly. Here was the right person to bring up, and, if necessary, to protect, the worse than orphan child.

"Yes, I know him," was all Miss Grogan said of Halbert Trevena. "I agree with you; the best thing we can do for Nanny is never to mention her father's name, 'Non ragionam de lor, ma guarda e passa,'" added she, with a little innocent pedantry—she was evidently a well-educated woman. And so the subject ended.

For a long time the godmother refused to accept any money for Nanny, but finally her Irish pride had to submit to her evidently narrow means, and the practical common sense of Mrs. Trevena; and it was agreed that a fair annual payment should be guaranteed by Nanny's uncle and aunt, if they both lived.

"And if we die," said Susannah, "there is still this diamond ring."

"I know it of old."

"He says it is 'of no particular value.'"

"Let us find out," was the answer, with a smile, that might have been called sarcastic, had not Miss Grogan been such a very pleasant old lady.

So the two elders went—the two children following—down into the pleasant streets of Bath, to a jeweler's there, and found that the diamond, though roughly set, was of great value—probably worth three or four hundred pounds.

Susannah breathed with new relief and thankfulness.

"Then, in any case, the child will not be destitute. Should we die before she is grown up, it will suffice to educate her. Do you hear, Nanny?" for she felt it better that the child, who knew so much, should know everything. "This ring is yours, your grandfather's gift: it is worth several hundred pounds, and you shall have it when you are twenty-one, or when you marry."

"I don't mean to marry—mamma told me not—it would only make me miserable," said the child, her tears beginning to flow, as they always did when she spoke of her mother; but the consoler was at hand. She turned to him gratefully—"Yes, I think I will marry—I'll marry you, Cousin Arthur—and then you will get the diamond ring."

Arthur blushed—schoolboy fashion; and Miss Grogan said primly, "My dear, you are too young to talk about such things." Mrs. Trevena said nothing, but was conscious of a queer sensation, scarcely an arrow—

more like a pin-prick—at her heart, for which she laughed at herself, but did not get rid of it—not for days.

She left Nanny quite content, for her godmother was evidently well remembered by her; and there had appeared at tea-time two little girls, Australian-born, who had been confided to Miss Grogan for education. These young companions lessened the grief of parting with Arthur: and Arthur himself seemed to feel he had done his utmost duty to "only a girl," and might now plunge back into boy-life, and tell his mother all about the delight of Winchester.

No tongue can tell the relief it was when Susannah found herself sitting in the rectory parlor—alone with her very own two, her husband and son, and nobody else! The storm had come and gone; she had borne it, had done her duty through it—her utmost duty—and now the sky was clear, at least for a time.

Alas, no! When Arthur went to bed she told her husband as much as it seemed desirable to tell about little Nanny's affairs, to which Mr. Trevena listened with his usual absent-mindedness. The worried look gradually returned to his face; till at last, when Susannah asked the natural question, "Any letters?" he drew one out of his pocket. It was the long-familiar handwriting that always foreboded trouble.

"This came yesterday, but I would not answer it till you returned home. Read it, and tell me what you think."

It was one of those lucky chances which few men's lives are quite without; which had come again and again to Halbert Trevena, and been thrown away. An old friend of the family, whom he had just met accidentally, after having lost sight of for years, had offered him a situation abroad, at a tea-garden in Ceylon; a *bona fide* offer, for he inclosed the letter in which it was made—a most kind letter from an old man, who knew scarcely anything of him, except that he was a Trevena. It seemed to have touched that callous heart. Though there would be hard work and little pay, Hal wished to accept the situation, and asked his brother "for really the last time" to assist him; to pay his passage and give him a small outfit to begin "a new life in a new land."

"He may prosper there, he is so clever," said Austin. "And not very old—only a year older than I." Indeed he looked much younger, having such a splendid physique, and what some cynical physician has called the secret of long life—" a good digestion, and no heart to speak of." "Who knows, Susannah, but that poor Hal might do well yet?"

Susannah, loath to wound this pathetic, lingering, fraternal love, replied that it was "just possible." At any rate, she felt that some sacrifice was worth making, if only to get rid of him.

So the money was sent, though not in coin, the passage being paid to the ship's agent, and the outfitter's bill ordered to be forwarded to the rectory: precautions not unnecessary. Hal did not resent them; he never resented anything, and always accepted everything. About his daughter he asked not a single question; nor even named her, until his farewell letter, when, apologizing for having no time to come to Tawton, he said that he left her "with entire confidence" to the care of her uncle and aunt.

"Poor fellow! Perhaps I may never set eyes on him again—the climate of Ceylon is very bad, they say. Would there be any chance of seeing him off from Southampton?"

There was a pathos in Mr. Trevena's look which his wife could not resist. Much as it often irritated her, she could not but see, with a tenderness approaching to reverence, how deep in this good man's heart lay that divine charity which "believeth all things—hopeth all things." The journey would be a trouble and expense, and the family finances were already sorely strained—would be more so by the payment for Nanny. Not for Arthur: oh! with what glad pride did she reflect that Arthur's education would cost Mr. Trevena almost nothing. She calculated a little, and then said:

"If you like, Austin, we will go to Southampton at once."

"You too?" he said joyfully. And they started: their first journey together for many a long year. It felt almost like a honeymoon.

Susannah had almost expected not to see her brother-in-law—but he was there. He seemed really to have "turned over a new leaf"—as people say—though alas! the new leaf often gets as blurred and blotted as the old one! He met them with even more than his customary *empressement*, and the trio had a peaceful and pleasant dinner together at the hotel before joining that company, sad and strange—which goes on board every P. and O. steamer with last farewells.

Their adieux were, however, no heart-break to any one. Captain Trevena was in exuberant spirits. The newly-made widower might have been a gay young bachelor beginning the world, free as air, with not a cloud of regret or remorse upon his heart.

"How is Nanny?" he did once ask; but he never waited for the answer; and soon after said—quite carelessly as it seemed: "By the bye, have you brought the little ring I wished for?—not that it is worth much, but I should like to wear it in memory of my late dear wife."

For an instant Susannah was silent with indignant contempt; then she said, in a manner that he could not mistake:

"I know exactly what the ring is worth, for I have had it valued by a jeweler. But it is not yours—it is Nanny's—left her by her grandfather. I shall keep it for her till she is twenty-one."

"The devil you will!" And truly the devil himself glared out of the angry eyes, and spoke in the muttered execration which followed. But Captain Trevena had been checkmated—or rather he had checkmated himself: and it was too late now, except for furious looks and words, which fell harmless upon the little woman before him. He might as well have stormed against a stone—and he knew it.

However, he thought it wiser to let all pass. His handsome face recovered its usual bland smile, and by the time that "All on shore" was called out, he was ready with a cheery good-bye.

"It really was most kind of you, Austin, to come and see me off. Give my love to Nanny. Say, I leave her in charge of the best of uncles—and aunts ".(with a bow in which it was difficult to say whether politeness or sarcasm predominated). " Good-bye to you both—good-bye."

They left him kissing his hand to them as he leant over the ship's side; but almost before Susannah ventured to speak to her husband, who had turned aside, the tears running down his cheeks, she saw Halbert laughing and talking with some ladies: he had already made acquaintance with several of the passengers, and before reaching Suez would doubtless be the most popular man on board.

"No need to grieve for him," she thought, but said nothing. Nor did her husband. All the under tragedies of life are often acted—and perhaps best—in total silence.

"Hal may do well yet," Mr. Trevena said, as a sort of remorseful balance-weight against the deep sense of relief that they both felt in coming back, they two alone, to their peaceful home. Except for that grave, equally peaceful, in the churchyard hard by, all the last weeks might have been a painful dream. Once more the rector and his wife sauntered leisurely up and down the peach-tree walk, and Arthur went back to his lessons, and was for ever asking his papa about old Winchester days— which the old Wykehamite recalled with utmost enthusiasm—the days " when Hal and I were boys together;" only one was an idler and the other a worker. Still— Austin often ended with the sigh—" But Hal may do well yet."

He might have done—though it is seldom that at the eleventh hour the Ethiopian changes his skin and the leopard his spots—but fate—cruel or merciful, who dare say!—ordained it otherwise.

Three days after he sailed the daily newspaper brought to the rectory, and to many another English home, tidings of one of those disasters at sea, which not seldom happen to outward-bound ships—a collision in the channel. The emigrant ship—a miserable unseaworthy craft—went down immediately, but the passengers and crew of the large steamer did their best to save all the lives they could, launching boats, and helping the drowning wretches to climb on board. One passenger in particular, it was said, had assisted many, holding on at the ship's side, and throwing out from thence ropes and life-preservers. But the vessel gave a lurch—he fell overboard—and never rose again. The name of this brave passenger, it was ascertained, was Halbert Trevena.

So all was over. No more hope—nor fear. His death, more honorable than ever his life had been, covered over its many shortcomings—or sins. "Captain Trevena's heroic conduct" was mentioned in the newspapers: and for months after, letters of condolence, admiration, and gratitude, reached the rectory from friends and strangers. No one could have desired a more lauded or lamented end.

Scarcely a melancholy end, Susannah sometimes thought. For his last act had been perhaps the noblest in his life. Better he should die as he did, and when he did, and be spoken of with praise and remembered with tenderness. She thought, with untold thankfulness, of that journey to Southampton, and how the brothers had parted in peace, with kindly good wishes, hopes and prayers—which perhaps Heaven had answered in its own way.

There was no need to go and console Nanny for the death of a parent who had never been such to her except in name;—but Mrs. Trevena collected carefully all that the newspapers had said in his praise, and every letter which reached the rectory concerning him, asking Miss Grogan to keep them for Nanny, and teach the child to forget everything about her father except his blameless and heroic end.

CHAPTER VI

Young lovers are a sweet and pleasant sight: and so are young married people, absorbed in their present bliss, with the future stretching out before them, all in a golden haze. But the sweetest and sacredest sight of all is an elderly couple to whom hope has become certainty: whose future has narrowed down to a quiet present—yet who love one another still, and by the strength and perfectness of that love are able to enjoy Now, without regretting Then.

Thus it was with Mr. and Mrs. Trevena. Though married late in life, their real union had begun so early, that neither had a past or desired a future in which the other had no share. Of course, their felicity had not been unclouded: what human happiness is? But " the little rift within the lute "—which happens in almost all marriages, and has power in many to " make the music mute "—had been closed by wise hands; partly the hand of Providence, and partly—let it be honestly said!— their own. There is no marriage which cannot be made unhappy—there are few marriages which cannot be made less unhappy—if the parties concerned so choose.

Austin and Susannah had not grown less happy as they grew older—rather the contrary. He no longer sacrificed everything, his wife included, on the shrine of what is called "family duty"—a religion which, begun in the noblest faith, sometimes degenerates into a mere fetish-worship of what is essentially mean and base. And Susannah, when, also out of duty, she let her boy become a schoolboy, and contented herself with only seeing him in the holidays—was saved from that passion of maternal idolatry which might have proved equally fatal for him, for her, and for her husband. Gradually she learnt the inevitable lesson of all mothers—to sit still and see their children happy on their own account. Not ceasing to make them happy, but ceasing to feel wounded because the new generation has a happiness apart from the old.

When Arthur's letters came, brimful of enjoyment,— Greek and football, cricket, music, and mathematics being inextricably muddled up together—for the young "King" verified the adage of "good at work, good at play"; full too of Winchester slang, which Mr. Trevena recalled with delight, and protested was not vulgar at all, but only archaic and historical—the unexacting mother read the brief postscript—"How are you all at home?" and did not expect more. She knew her darling loved her in his heart; and that the thirteen years during which she had had him all to herself, to train both mind and body in the right way, would never be lost, but bear fruit in time to come.

Yet when he returned, after a few months, a regular Winchester boy, at first he seemed something new and strange. He had grown very tall; and, it could not be denied, promised to be extremely handsome: even though he had cropped his curly hair in the cruellest way, and scarred his long slender hands with knife-cuts; nay, as he told his mother with great pride, had been within an inch of breaking his beautiful Roman nose. Still, despite these drawbacks, when he went to church with her the first Sunday, he was a boy that most people would have turned round to look at, and whom any mother would be proud to have standing by her side, and singing away—" like a cherubim "—one old woman in the congregation said—with the waning beauty of his boyish voice, which had made him already notable in the Winchester choir.

" Whether or not Arthur will turn out handsome, he certainly looks every inch a gentleman," she said to her husband as they took their peaceful stroll between services, up and down the peach-tree walk.

" All Wykehamites are gentlemen," the rector answered with pardonable prejudice.

But she had meant something more than that. "What is bred in the bone will come out in the flesh"—is a truth which there is no gainsaying. All the education in the world would never have put into Arthur what did not inherently exist there. There must have been good material, natural or hereditary, to work upon. Now, far more than when he was a baby—her own innocent, helpless baby—did Susannah speculate about him, noticing every new development, and contrasting him with other children. Especially with Nanny, who shortly after also came home for the holidays.

The "last of the Trevenas," as her uncle sometimes pathetically called her, was, Mrs. Trevena thought, very inferior to her own Arthur. Nanny was a good little girl; but she was prim and quiet, taciturn and plain. She could not compare at all with the big schoolboy—full of life, health, and activity. Not that Arthur was ever unkind to her; but he just ignored her, as schoolboys do ignore little girls, unless specially attractive. He tried to be civil and polite—brought her flowers and condescendingly took her a walk now and then; but he told his mother confidentially that "Nanny was a big baby"—and escaped from her society whenever he politely could. At which poor Nanny used to look so miserable, that Mrs. Trevena considered seriously whether it would not be better in future to arrange the child's home-coming at a different time from Arthur's.

But next year Fate took the decision out of her hands; for Miss Grogan had a severe illness, and Nanny, with a resolution which her uncle and aunt had not expected in so small a child, absolutely refused to leave her.

"Nanny always was a devoted little creature," said Mrs. Trevena, remembering those few days in the sickroom—the room of death. But still she was not sorry to have her boy all to herself for those brief, too brief holiday weeks; when she could watch him growing up to manhood—the delight of her heart—the desire of her eyes.

He was in truth a very fine young fellow. At sixteen he was little short of six feet high. Slender and supple as a willow-wand, yet not lanky; very muscular and strong for his age. He was good at all athletic sports, and made as much use of his body as he did of his brains. His mother's maxim, "Better to wear out than rust out," seemed exemplified in "King" Arthur—though he did not seem likely to wear out for the next threescore years at least; for the wholesome upbringing of his childhood had resulted in a healthy youth, and bade fair to develop into a splendid manhood.

Often when she looked at him, she wondered whence all this came—this wealth of physical and mental power; much as Merlin must have wondered, when he saw grow up under his eyes the "little naked child;" naked of every hereditary blessing; owing fortune nothing—not even a name.

"The boys always call you Trevena?" she once said to him anxiously. "They—they ask no questions?"

Arthur blushed, as he had done more than once lately when strangers made unconscious ignorant remarks; such as noticing his height, and saying he "took after his papa."

"They did chaff me at first, mother—just a little. And one fellow called me Nemo—but I thrashed him to within an inch of his life. And then I told the other fellows the plain truth about myself, as you advised me. Nobody ever said an ill word to me afterwards."

So, already had begun for Arthur that battle with the world, from which his mother could not defend him—she could only give him strength for the conflict.

"That was well," she answered gently. "Indeed, I think only a 'sneak' or a 'cad,' as you call them, would have been unkind to you. A name and even a family are not worth much sometimes—were not to poor little Sir Eustace Damerel, who died last Christmas. We shall see what the new Damerels will be like. They came to

Tawton Abbas last week, and will likely be at church next Sunday."

Thus said she, to turn away her boy's thoughts from himself. But she need not have feared—Arthur's nature was too wholesome, and his youth too full of hope and brightness, to have any morbid or sentimental feelings about either his origin or his future lot. And Winchester had not made him oblivious of Tawton Magna. He took the vividest interest in hearing about the Damerels—Sir Charles and his lady; who had inherited the title and estates, and come to reside at the great house—which, being the only house except farm-houses for miles round, was a matter of some importance to the rectory.

"Do you mean to call there, mother? You ought," said Arthur—who was a little given to laying down the law—as is not uncommon at sixteen. "Are they young folks or old? Have they got any children?"

"I believe they are rather elderly people; distant cousins, whom nobody ever heard about till lately. And I think, but I am not sure—they have no children."

At which Arthur's interest died down—he said he didn't care for "old fogies." And next Sunday he scarcely glanced in the direction of the Tawton Abbas pew, where, in the two arm-chairs which had stood there for generations back, sat the new Baronet and Lady Damerel. They sat, with dead Damerels underfoot and monuments to the same overhead—the last representatives of the race. Only their two selves; though report declared they had had several children—all dead now. Susannah wondered how a childless couple should ever have cared to claim either title or property.

7

Of course they were stared at eagerly by the whole congregation. A curious pair—she, a fine-looking, fashionable woman, with a complexion much too fair and hair much too dark for her age; but the simple villagers suspected nothing, and set her down as being younger than her husband, who was a feeble-looking, melancholy little man, nigh upon seventy. Two footmen had helped him into church, and set him in his chair, whence he never moved, for his feet and hands were all knotted and distorted with rheumatism. But he had a mild and not unpleasing face—aristocratic—aquiline—"as big a nose as mine," Arthur said, in commenting upon them after church. "But oh! I wouldn't be Sir Charles Damerel for the world!"

"Nor I Lady Damerel," said Mrs. Trevena. "Poor woman—what an unhappy face! No wonder, if she has lost all her children."

And Susannah almost regretted having stopped to speak to them at the church door, introducing herself as the rector's wife, and Arthur as "my son." "How she must envy me!" thought the tender-hearted soul, and blamed herself for flaunting before the childless woman her own superior bliss.

"I don't think Lady Damerel's children could have been very fond of her," remarked Arthur sententiously. "She may be good-looking, but she has the hardest and most unpleasant face I ever saw. My little mammy is worth a hundred of her," added he, putting his arm round his mother's waist as of old; he was now growing past the age when boys are ashamed of their mothers, and he petted and patronized her to her heart's content.

Still, he was too much of the schoolboy to care to "go about visiting," and absolutely declined—unless she particularly wished it—to accompany her to Tawton Abbas, or make acquaintance with that "horrid old couple;" over whom she had such unnecessary compassion that even the rector smiled.

"My dear Susannah, I can't see that Lady Damerel needs the least pity—or desires it. I hear she is a most accomplished woman; will fill the house with brilliant society, and be popular everywhere. The rector's wife will be nobody—the squire's wife will take the shine out of you completely."

"I'd like to see it!" cried Arthur, blazing up; "I'd like to find the lady who was fit to hold a candle to *my* mother!" he continued, dragging forward the easiest arm-chair and putting her into it, and waiting upon her unremittingly during their pleasant Sunday supper, when all the servants were out, and Arthur did everything. He had that happy knack of true gentlemanhood, never to be ashamed of doing everything—or anything: always ready to notice every one's need, and supply it—especially his mother's.

"You are my eyes, my hands, and my feet," she sometimes said to the boy; and gave herself up, more and more every holidays, to the delight of being dependent—of leaning on her big son, with a sort of triumphant weakness that was utmost joy.

But he was an obstinate young monkey for all his good qualities; possessing strongly the violent likes and dislikes of youth. And so it happened that for two whole years he never crossed the threshold of Tawton Abbas.

K

Nor did the rector and his wife very often—not oftener than politeness and their position demanded. Susannah had few interests in common with the fashionable woman of the world, who was afraid of growing old, and who seemed to have no youth to remember; at least she never mentioned it. Austin, too, had little sympathy with Sir Charles, who, though gentle and gentlemanly, did not seem to have two ideas in his head—read no books, took no special interest in anything, and seemed mortally in fear of his clever wife. She on her part noticed him very little, and led a regular society-life—at least as gay a one as she could accomplish—going to London whenever she could, and bringing London people down with her on every possible occasion. But she mixed very little with the neighboring families, who, being unable to discover her antecedents (Sir Charles's, of course, were patent—he was a Damerel and that was enough), concluded there was "something odd" about her. Perhaps, as she had some slight accent, not quite English, and spoke several continental tongues, she was a foreigner—never much approved of in provincial society. Still, she was very handsome—very lady-like; all the gentlemen admired her, but the ladies thought her "not domestic," and wondered that at her age she should care for concerts, private theatricals, and the like.

However, to their opinion of her Lady Damerel seemed wholly indifferent. She gave a tenants' ball at Christmas, and a garden-party, to all classes not lower than doctors and lawyers, every summer. But beyond that the village and the rectory saw almost nothing of her, except at church, which she attended regularly, and where Mrs. Trevena, tender-hearted still, often compassionated the discontented look and restless manner of the rich, clever, prosperous woman, who had neither son nor daughter—not even niece or nephew—at her empty fireside.

"How very empty it must be when the visitors go, and Sir Charles and she are left alone," Susannah said one day. "I think I will really pluck up heart; go and call at Tawton Abbas, and take Nanny with me." Nanny happened to be staying for a fortnight at the rectory, and her uncle and aunt had found her so harmless, even pleasant in the house, that they had kept her for a month. But the call resulted in nothing—not even an invitation to tea for the quiet unimpressive little maiden, who was stared at from the piercing black eyes, through a double *pince-nez*.

"Miss Trevena—did you say? Your daughter, I conclude?"

"My niece; I have no daughter. It is my son you see at church, Lady Damerel."

"Oh yes, I remember now. A tall young fellow—rather good-looking. You must bring him to see me some day. But we have no young people here, Miss Trevena. Your mother—I mean your aunt—is more fortunate than I. All my children are dead."

She said this, not with any tone of regret, but simply as stating a fact; then proceeded to discuss a new book and a new opera; talking miles above the head of poor innocent Nanny, who thought that cousin Arthur—whom she seemed to miss extremely from the rectory in spite of his ignoring of her—was right in considering

Lady Damerel the finest of fine ladies, and the most unpleasant.

Nanny was now getting old enough for her future to require consideration. Not from her uncle, who never looked a day ahead: but she and her aunt sometimes talked it over. Nanny was an independent little soul. She knew she had not a penny in the world; except the value of that diamond ring; nor a friend, save Miss Grogan, who was growing old and frail. Perhaps her mother's sore experience still lingered in her little soul —for she was not a bit of a Trevena, nor seemed much drawn to the Trevenas. She said calmly, "I shall be a governess;" and though very grateful to her uncle for all his goodness, made it clear enough that as soon as she could earn her own bread, she would never eat the bread of dependence. Her aunt saw, not without thankfulness, that Halbert Trevena's daughter was, as often happens, the very opposite of himself. But though she was very kind to Nanny, and liked her sincerely, she scarcely loved her—one cannot make oneself love even a child. And then all her heart was bound up in her own boy. When Nanny went away, and Arthur came home for the holidays, Susannah felt the difference.

"King" Arthur was much altered—much improved. He was in his last year at Winchester, and looked quite the young man. There had never been much of the "hobbledehoy" in him, probably because he was not shy—he did not think enough about himself for shyness. Reserved he was, in a sense; but that painful bashfulness, which as often springs from egotism as modesty, never troubled him much. By nature—and also by wise upbringing—he was a complete altruist—always interested in other people, and "bothering" himself very little about himself and his own affairs.

But just now he could hardly help it. He had come home greatly excited by an incident—a coincidence such as happens in real life oftener than we think, and yet when put into books everybody cries out, "How unnatural!"

One day a little "commoner" he knew was visited by a hitherto unknown grandfather, whom all the boys were inclined to laugh at, for his strong American accent and queer American ways, till they found out what a kindly old fellow he was, and what funny stories he told.

"He tipped us all round and asked our names, and when he heard mine, he started as if I'd hit him. Who do you think he was mother? Guess now—guess?"

It needed no guessing. "Dr. Franklin! I am so glad he is alive."

"Very much alive, indeed!" cried Arthur. "He's as sharp and clever as ever he can be; and so kind—all the fellows liked him, though he was a foreigner and an American. I'm not a bit ashamed of my godfather; and I like him very much."

"You have need to," said Susannah gravely. And when a few days after Dr. Franklin appeared at the rectory ("as large as life and twice as natural," said he, with his queer internal chuckle), the welcome he received was almost pathetic in its earnestness. When Susannah sat talking to him, and found him scarcely changed—as gaunt and lanky, quaint and kind, as ever—it seemed as if eighteen years were rolled away like a cloud, and she were once more the woman who sat beneath the snow-wall above Andermatt—gazing on the snow-mountains, and trying not to be broken-hearted, but to accept God's will whatever it was, and make for herself a happy life—unconscious how even then that Holy Will was preparing for her a happiness she never dreamt of.

"Look at him," she said, as Arthur just then crossed the lawn with his two big dogs, whistling to them, and then breaking out into a stave of "Dulce domum," in a voice which promised to be a fine tenor some day. "Who would have thought my baby—your baby, doctor, you saved him for me! would have grown up to that!"

"It's a trick they have, ma'am. My ten are all men and women now—uncommonly good-looking too, some of them."

And then he explained that his eldest daughter—"fine girl—very fine—took after her mother, not me"—had married a rich English baronet, which accounted for the fact of himself being grandfather to a Winchester boy.

"Your boy might be a baronet's son too, ma'am, if there's anything in blood. Mrs. Franklin says there isn't; that it's all upbringing. But in that case even, Arthur does you the greatest credit."

"Thank you," said Susannah; and then tacitly following the young fellow—for it seemed such a pleasure to look at him—they passed through the churchyard into the park of Tawton Abbas; still talking like old friends, and regretting that a very natural incident—Dr. Franklin's losing their address, and therefore being unable to give them his own—had made them strangers for so many years.

"Which have been happy years, by your looks, Mrs. Trevena? No anxiety over your boy?—you have never heard anything about that woman?" Dr. Franklin did not say that "mother"—who had no right to the name.

"Never. Have you?"

Dr. Franklin looked uncomfortable. "I did not mean to tell you unless you asked me the direct question; but—she has bothered me a little. At least I suppose it was she."

And then he explained that a year or two ago there had appeared in a New York paper an advertisement for a Dr. Franklin, who would "hear of something to his advantage," which his wife had insisted on his answering; and then had come a letter, in an evidently feigned hand, requesting particulars about a child that was born at Andermatt—whether "it" was alive—and where "it" was?

"Perhaps she had forgotten whether 'it' was a boy or a girl. 'Can a mother forget her sucking child?'—Well—some mothers do."

"And what did you reply?" Mrs. Trevena could scarcely speak for agitation.

"Least said, soonest mended—I never answered one single word."

"Thank you—thank you! Did you keep the letter? What address was given?"

"Mrs. Franklin has it. Some milliner or dressmaker, I think, in London."

"In London!" A shudder of repulsion and dread

7*

passed over Susannah; and then that stern sense of justice, so strong in her, conquered it. "Perhaps she was a dressmaker—some poor working-woman who was almost starving, and did not wish her baby to starve too."

"Pshaw!—Does that boy look like the son of a working-woman? And it was herself she wanted to save from starvation, not her baby. No, no, ma'am; I saw her—you never did. She used always to rave about being a 'woman of genius'—very likely an actress or singer—that very singer who ran away from Milan."

"I have sometimes thought so. And the musical faculty descends. Just listen to that boy."

Arthur was singing "Dulce domum" at the top of his voice—a rather cracked voice now; but it was not ignorant singing—he evidently knew what he was about.

"Music is his passion, as it is with many a boy, till the work of the world knocks it out of him. But this letter—Stop, there is the Tawton Abbas carriage—let us step aside."

For Mrs. Trevena felt that to interchange polite nothings with the great lady would, at this moment, be beyond her power. She and Dr. Franklin passed under a group of trees, so that Lady Damerel never saw them.

Arthur, however, did not step aside. He ceased his gay school-song, and standing on the grass, lifted his hat, as the carriage drove by, with a gesture so carelessly graceful, so unlike country youths in general, that Lady Damerel turned to look after him.

He was, in truth, worth looking at, in his rough gray

clothes, with a gray cap set on the top of his crisp fair curls—it was before the time when the fashion made young men crop themselves like returned convicts. Lithe and slender as a young David, and in manner neither shy nor forward, because thinking more of other people than himself—Arthur never came to, and had now quite passed, that awkward stage when a boy does not know what to do with himself, and especially with his legs and arms.

It was no wonder, Mrs. Trevena thought, that Lady Damerel, indifferent as she was to her neighbors, should turn and glance after him.

"Poor woman!" said she, explaining to Dr. Franklin a little of the domestic history of Tawton Abbas. "I dare say she would give the world to have a son like mine."

"Maybe. But there are mothers—and mothers, like the woman we were talking about. Shall I tell Mrs. Franklin to send you her letter? if she hasn't burnt it, which perhaps may have been the best thing."

"Perhaps," echoed Susannah, wishing in her heart—though her conscience reproached her—that it might be burnt, and forgotten. "It could do no good to Arthur."

"No, for the lad doesn't care a straw about his mother."

"I am his mother," said Susannah, with a certain grave dignity.

"You're right, ma'am. May he never have any other as long as he lives!"

But mothers, even the happiest mothers of the best of sons, have their anxieties.

Some days after this, Dr. Franklin, with the practical common sense of a man of the world, asked his godson, very naturally, what he was going to be?

Arthur hesitated, and looked uncomfortable. His mother, thinking this arose from diffidence or modesty, answered for him.

"My son's career is already cut out for him. There are six New College scholarships given at Winchester every year. Arthur is so good at mathematics, the head-master tells us, that he is quite sure of one. He will go in for it next year and take himself to college as he did to school. Then—a boy who has earned his own education can generally earn his own living; especially at Oxford."

"But, mother," said Arthur slowly, "I may not go to Oxford at all. I mean to be a musician."

"A what?" cried Dr. Franklin, bursting into laughter. "A street-singer, or an organ-grinder, going about the country with a monkey and a couple of white mice!"

Ridicule is the sharpest of weapons with the young. Arthur turned white with anger, but controlled himself, and explained that a friend of his, just returned from a German Conservatoire, had advised him to go there and study music as a profession.

"At whose expense, my boy?" asked Dr. Franklin, dryly.

Arthur colored. "I don't know. I have never thought."

"But you ought to think—you are old enough. How old?"

"Eighteen past. Next year I should go in for the scholarship, if I go in at all. Mother?"

She did not answer. It was the first time she had heard of this idea; the first time her boy had kept back anything from her, or that his will had run counter to hers, never an arbitrary will. From his very childhood, as soon as he could reason at all, she had taught him to use his reason, and had never from him exacted blind obedience. Explanation, whenever possible, she gave; and her argument was never "Do it because I command it," but "Do it because it is right."

This fancy of Arthur's struck her with sharp pain.

No wonder she looked sad and grave—and even the second anxious appeal—"What do you say, mother?" brought no response. Just then Mr. Trevena was heard calling all over the house, "Susannah—Susannah!"—as he usually did if he missed her for five minutes, and she hurried away without having said a word.

"Well, young man? You are a nice young man, to make your mother look like that! Still nicer to expect your father to maintain you in expensive study for the next five or ten years."

Arthur flushed crimson. He liked his godfather sincerely; still, Dr. Franklin often "rubbed him up the wrong way." It was the contrast between the practical and the artistic temperament; the born democrat, and —well, heaven only knew what Arthur's birth was, but he looked the young "aristocrat," every inch of him.

"I don't know what you mean," he said. "I had no idea of vexing my mother; and I wish to stand on my own feet as soon as ever I can."

"That's right, lad. I did it, before I was your age. I was message-boy at a chemist's store. But I soon went ahead—we all go ahead in the States. Our motto is 'Every man for himself, and'—taking off his cap reverently—'God for us all.' That's what I said to my six sons," continued he. "I gave them a good education, and then I left them to shift for themselves. And they have done it—uncommonly well, too. There isn't one of them now that ever wants a cent from his father."

"I hope I shall not from mine—at least, not for very long," said Arthur, proudly.

"That's right, my boy; for Mr. Trevena isn't as young as he has been, and he has another encumbrance besides yourself—that little girl your mother told me of. What's her name?"

"Nanny."

"I hear she's a plucky little thing, and means to go out as a governess—which is quite right. A woman should earn her own bread as well as a man. But if her uncle helped anybody, he ought to help her; because, you see, she is his own flesh and blood, and you——"

"I understand!" And again came that violent blush, which showed what keen sensitiveness lurked under Arthur's merry and manly outside. Then, speaking with evident effort, "Godfather, you are right to remind me of that. Tell me—for I believe you were present at my birth—who were my father and mother?"

"My poor lad, I declare to you I haven't the slightest idea."

They had gone outside the drawing-room window, and were lying on the grassy slope—the Kentuckian puffing at his pipe, and Arthur sitting beside him, his arms round his knees, gazing straight forward, with a graver expression than his wont. Dr. Franklin scanned him sharply.

"It was an awkward business, Arthur. If I were you, I'd think about it as little as possible."

"So I do. As mother often says, a man is responsible for himself and his children, but certainly not for his parents. Still, I should like to know all I can."

"How much has your mother told you?"

"Only that you found me—you and she—somewhere in the Alps. I suppose I had a father and a mother, but she never speaks of them at all."

"Bravo!" muttered Dr. Franklin. But he himself felt no inclination for such generous reticence; he thought it fairer on all sides that the boy should know everything; so he then and there told him everything.

Arthur listened, his cap drawn over his eyes, his hands—such long, slender, beautiful hands—clasped together round his knees.

"Thank you," he said at last. "I am glad I know. The—the lady—was, you suppose, an opera-singer?"

"I don't say that, but it's possible."

"And she sold me, you say—sold me for twenty pounds?"

"Yes." He was just on the point of adding, "and she'd like to buy you back again now," when he remembered Mrs. Trevena's caution, that until they heard from America they should say nothing about the letter. It would not benefit Arthur—perhaps only unsettle him. And they had the dressmaker's address; while the unmotherly mother—her brief note, if hers, was, Dr. Franklin declared, "as cold as a stone"—had to them no clue whatever. "All the better!" thought he. And Mr. and Mrs. Trevena just then appearing, he ended the conversation.

It was not renewed; though he stayed some days longer at the rectory. The annual garden-party at Tawton Abbas was coming off, and the old Kentuckian said he should like to "study life" in an English country-house. So in addition to the invitation for "Mr. and Mrs. Trevena, and Mr. Trevena, junior"—("you see, mother"—laughed Arthur—"your fine lady doesn't even take the trouble to discover my Christian name")—a note was sent to Tawton Abbas for permission to bring "a friend from America" to join the party.

"Then you'll not want me," said Arthur, very reluctant to go. But his mother wished it. He had been unlike himself, she thought, the last day or two; and though she had carefully abstained from reviving the Oxford question till Dr. Franklin was gone, still she saw that something was on his mind. He followed her about with extra tenderness, divining all she wanted, and doing everything for her more like a girl than a boy. But he said nothing until they were walking together across the park to the garden-party; only they two, for Dr. Franklin had home letters to write by the mail, and he and Mr. Trevena could not appear till late.

So Susannah had her boy all to herself; and very nice he looked, and very proud she was of him. He was proud of her too, he said, after eying her over with the sharp criticism of youth—approving her new dress, and wishing she would wear it every day.

"But I can't afford silk every day," said she, laughing. "I am not Lady Damerel."

"No, thank goodness! I wouldn't change my little mother for a dozen Lady Damerels."

"Well, then, I'll try to dress a little better and talk a little more, just to please you and papa. I am glad my son is not ashamed of me."

"I hope my mother is not ashamed of me," said Arthur gravely. And then he told her in a few words —so few that it was easy to see how deeply he felt—of the conversation between his godfather and himself; and how he had made up his mind to go in for mathematics and give up music entirely.

Susannah breathed a sigh of thankfulness, and then replied, "Not entirely, my son. Music may still be your pleasure—your staff, if not your crutch."

"Not at present. I love it so that I must give it up, if I mean to be anything. And I do mean to be something, some day," added he, tossing his head and planting his foot firmly on the ground.

The young think the old were never young. It did not occur to Arthur that his quiet little mother felt her heart throb while he spoke. She too had had her dreams—of fame, ambition, love—had written verses by the yard and stories by the dozen; yet she had earned her bread as a daily governess, and finally would end her days as the old wife of a country parson. But she had eaten cheerfully the dry bread of existence, and made it sweet by thankfulness. Though tears were in her eyes now, they were not regretful tears.

"I think, Arthur, you are right. The secret of life is

not to do what one likes, but to try to like that which one has to do. And one does come to like it—in time."

"Yes, mother. And if I turn out a great Oxford don—shall you be pleased? Would you like me to make a name for myself?—the only name I've got," added he with a slight bitterness of tone, which went to Susannah's heart. "So I'll go in for the scholarship at New College, and papa need not spend a halfpenny upon me at Oxford. Then—poor little Nanny need not be a governess."

"What made you think of Nanny?" asked Mrs. Trevena with some surprise. For the children had scarcely met for years, until last week, and then only for a few hours; since Arthur came home at night, and Nanny left next morning. She had been very shy with him, and he had treated her with the majestic bearing of a big boy towards a very little girl.

"My godfather said papa ought to help Nanny and not me. He is right; she is a girl—and she is papa's own."

"And you are my own!" answered Susannah, with the passionate tenderness that she so seldom expressed. But she said no more. The wisdom of parents sometimes lies in accepting rather than in making sacrifices.

Arther found himself less miserable than he had expected to be at the garden-party, even though it was, as some one graphically described, "a penn'orth of all sorts," through which the hostess moved like a condescending queen. She had various out-door amusements for the inferior folk—performing dogs, hand-bell ringers, etc.—and for her choicer guests there was very good music in the drawing-room. She looked politely surprised when she saw the Trevenas eagerly listening.

"Do you play or sing, Mrs. Trevena?"

"No, but my son does."

"Oh, indeed."

Here Mr. Hardy, the High Church curate, said a word or two, which caused the great lady to put up her *pince-nez* (she was old enough to wear spectacles, but never would) and scan Arthur sharply.

Most elderly women—mothers or not—like to look at a graceful handsome boy. As this childless woman did so, a vexed expression passed over her face—not regret or pain, but a sort of irritation. An outcry against Providence, Mrs. Trevena thought it was, and felt sorry for her, till Lady Damerel broke into the most gracious of careless smiles.

"Perhaps Mr. ——, I forget his Christian name,—Mr. Trevena will come to our rescue in accompanying a trio? Our own pianist has not come. And our soprano says she is too hoarse to sing. We are very unfortunate."

"Not if we can induce you to take her place," said some one near. "You know you have sung, Lady Damerel."

"Oh yes—a little—when I was a girl," said she carelessly, listening to the touch of Arthur's long fingers on the keys—the magic touch which all musicians recognize. It was a magnificent piano, and the artist's delight overcame the boy's shyness.

"Play something," she said; and Arthur played—exceedingly well. "Do you read at sight?"—and she placed the trio before him. It was one of those dashing operatic scenas of the last generation, full of show and difficulty, and embellished with *fioriture.* Arthur dashed into it—so did the tenor and bass—and finally, as if she could not help it, the soprano.

Lady Damerel must have had a fine voice once; and even now had the brilliant remains of it: a thoroughly cultivated voice—not tender, not pathetic, but high and flexible as a musical instrument, and capable of executing those wonderful *tours de force* which "bring the house down." She did it now; seeming quite to forget herself in the pleasure of her own performance: so much so that she thought necessary to apologize.

"I am almost too old to sing—but I used to like it once. Now—in my position—with my many social duties—of course a lady is different from a professional."

"You might have been a professional, ma'am: you sing so splendidly. I never heard anything better, even in America."

The honest Kentuckian had been standing outside the open French window, and now walked in—in his enthusiasm not waiting to be introduced. When Mr. Trevena mentioned "Dr. Franklin," Lady Damerel suddenly turned round.

"I guess you never saw an American before. And perhaps, ma'am, in my compliments to your singing, I was more honest than polite. But when we like a thing we also like to say so."

Lady Damerel bowed. She looked white—possibly with the exertion of singing.

"America's a fine country, ma'am, and we've some

uncommonly fine singers there—fine women too, especially in the South. You remind me of my countrywomen exceedingly."

Again Lady Damerel bowed, rather haughtily; and sat down, almost hiding her face with her large fan. But no blush came to her cheek except the permanent one which it owed to art: and she had the stereotyped smile of a person well used to flattery.

Mrs. Trevena, rather annoyed at her good friend's bluntness, took the first opportunity of getting him away —much to his amusement.

"I wanted to talk to Lady Damerel. She's an uncommonly handsome woman still, and very like an American. I wonder where she was raised. I'm sure I've seen her somewhere—or somebody very like her. Has she got a sister, do you know? And what sort of a fellow is the husband?"

Poor Sir Charles was meekly seated outside in his self-propelled chair; speaking to few people, and apparently very much afraid of everybody, especially his wife; for he kept out of her way as much as possible. Wreck as he was, he had a refined, amiable face—and stretched out a long feeble hand, knotted and distorted with rheumatism, to the stranger.

"Glad to see you—glad to see you—and so will my wife be. Lady Damerel is an American."

"Eh! why didn't she say so?" muttered the doctor; and, after a few words of civil conversation, went back to the drawing-room and watched her again. She sang no more, but stood talking, or rather listening, the centre of a group of talkers, with a polite absent smile, melting gradually into the weary dissatisfaction which was the permanent expression of her face whenever she ceased speaking.

"That isn't a happy woman, or a good woman," said the doctor to Mrs. Trevena.

"Perhaps if she were happy she might be good."

"I don't believe it. People make their own bed—nearly always—and as they make it they have to lie upon it. What a life she must have led that poor old fellow! Is she his second wife, do you think?"

"No. He once told my husband they had been married over thirty years, and had had four children—two boys first, and then two girls—all of whom are dead. She never cared for them, he said; but the poor old man seemed to have been fond of his children."

"I've seen her before—I'm certain I have," said Dr. Franklin meditatively, as he leant against the window outside; watching everybody and everything, but himself unobserved. "There, she has taken off her gloves. I always notice hands; they are as characteristic as faces. And what a diamond ring!"

The Kentuckian was beginning a whistle—a long, loud whistle of intense astonishment—but stopped himself.

"Good Lord! Yes. I was right. I *have* seen her before. It's the very woman."

"What woman?" asked Susannah innocently. She had drifted away from the subject, and become absorbed in weak contemplation—of her boy, of course! his graceful figure, his happy, handsome, interested face, as he stood talking to the tenor singer. In looking at him and thinking of his future—how soon he would be a man—and what a good, clever, noble man he was likely to be—a common delusion of mothers! she had entirely forgotten Lady Damerel.

"What woman, Mrs. Trevena?" echoed Dr. Franklin in a sharp whisper. "Why—that woman at Andermatt."

CHAPTER VII.

THERE is an old comedy entitled *The Wonder! A Woman keeps a Secret!* Its author could have known very little of human nature. How many secrets, not always their own, do women keep every day—out of love, or a sense of honor, or even pure pity! What wonderful strength they possess in hiding what they wish to hide! able to smile with a breaking heart—to wrap their robes smoothly and even gracefully over the beast that is gnawing their vitals. Men may be very good at concealment on some affairs—especially their own; but for absolute silence—years long—life long, if necessary—there is, in spite of the old dramatist, no secret-keeper like a woman.

When Dr. Franklin made the discovery of "the woman at Andermatt"—who, by the bye, must have kept her secret pretty well—Mrs. Trevena, startled as she was, had strength to whisper "Hush!"—for her husband was close behind them, and Arthur in front: and the good doctor had the sense to take the hint, and also to suggest that she was looking tired, and they had better go home.

"Make my excuses to Lady Damerel. She won't miss me very much," said he to the unconscious rector, and, tucking Mrs. Trevena under his arm, he walked away.

Not too soon. Susannah tottered blindly—almost without speaking a word—along the path which led to the rectory. But as soon as she got home she fainted outright.

However, it was too serious a crisis for any outward betrayal. Dr. Franklin brought her to herself without telling the servants, and by the time Mr. Trevena and Arthur came back, he and she had talked the whole thing calmly over, and made up their minds to keep it at present entirely between their two selves.

That the boy was Lady Damerel's son—her legitimate son—was more than possible—probable: but how was this to be proved? Not by herself—she dared not. Having concealed his birth so long—for Sir Charles, in speaking of his four children, was evidently quite ignorant that he had had a fifth child—to confess her folly, or wickedness, to the world and her husband, would entail an amount of scandal that few women could dare to brave. Born in wedlock the boy undoubtedly was; but what wife's fair fame could come out quite unspotted after such a disclosure?

"To run away from her husband—whether or not she went alone—to hide for months from him—to conceal her baby's birth and then sell it for twenty pounds—Phew!" said the doctor with his low, long whistle, which meant so much. "You are quite safe, ma'am. She'll never own her son—she dare not."

Susannah looked up. She had at first been utterly stunned—now there came upon her a sort of despair, or rather desperation—the blind fury which poets describe as that of "a lioness robbed of her whelps."

"He is my son—mine! No one has any right to him but me."

"That's true," answered Dr. Franklin soothingly. "And I doubt if Arthur would wish to have any mother but you. As for that woman there, she has tied up her own hands, cut her own throat, as one may say. He'd never care twopence for her. As for herself, it isn't a son she wants, it's an heir to the baronetcy. Let her be. It serves her right."

Such were the good doctor's arguments. Susannah's brain whirled so, that for a wonder she let another lead her, and did not attempt to think out the question for herself. When, two hours after, Arthur came in, bright and gay, having been exceedingly amused, especially by "that dreadful Lady Damerel—who is one big sham from top to toe—though she does sing so splendidly"— the whole thing seemed a ghastly nightmare, out of which she should wake soon and find it nothing.

Yet when she did wake next morning—after lying awake half the night—ah! well she understood those pathetic lines:—

> "The tears o' my heart fa' in showers frae my ee'
> While my gudeman sleeps soun' by me."

—then, Susannah found that yesterday had been not quite nothing. The mental agony, the perpetual self-restraint which it imposed, were so hard to bear that she was almost relieved when Dr. Franklin, who was obliged to leave next day, proposed taking his godson with him;

and Arthur, with a boy's natural delight at the idea of seeing London, was eager to go.

"But not if you want me, mother. I'll not go anywhere, or do anything, that you don't wish."

"I only wish what is for your good, my darling!" She had of late given up all pet names, knowing how schoolboys dislike them; but to-day she felt he was her darling—the very core of her heart, and the delight of her eyes—in whose future she had re-embarked many a ship-wrecked hope, many a broken dream. With difficulty she restrained herself from falling on Arthur's neck in a burst of bitter tears.

"It is for his good," said Dr. Franklin, with emphasis, and yet with a compassionate look in his kind eyes. "Give him a bit of pleasure with me, and then let him set to work. It's the best thing in the world for a lad to be obliged to work. Far better for him"—this was said with meaning and decision—"far better than if he were heir to a title and several thousands a year."

"Thank you—God bless you!" murmured Mrs. Trevena, as she wrung her friend's hand at parting; feeling that under his rough speech and queer un-English ways there lay hidden a heart of gold.

After a while, her agony of apprehension, her feeling that the whole world was slipping away from under her feet, slowly subsided. Life at the rectory went on as usual—nothing happened—nobody came. She did not see Lady Damerel at church, for Sir Charles had caught cold at the garden-party: an attack of rheumatism severer than ordinary had supervened; and the village heard, with little interest, that he and "my lady" had gone to Bath for several months. Tawton Abbas was shut up, and the rector and his wife wandered at ease about the lovely park—she with the strangest of feelings, and sometimes, in spite of what Dr. Franklin had said, with a doubt whether she were right or wrong in accepting the position of things, and letting all drift on in silence, as heretofore.

It may seem almost incredible, even in this simple-minded and unworldly woman—but the last thing she thought of was the worldly benefits—the title and estate to which her Arthur might be the lawful heir. Had he been proved the legitimate son of worthy parents, she could have given him up, she thought, though it broke her heart—but to give him up to such as Lady Damerel—never!

Better that he should begin life simply as an adopted son—work his own way in the world, and win a name for himself, for which he was indebted to nobody. Unworthy parents are worse than none.

Three months had gone by, and Arthur was just coming home for Christmas, after having worked "like a brick," he wrote, and being in cheerful hope of the scholarship—before Mrs. Trevena found herself again face to face with the woman whom she believed to be her boy's mother.

It happened in this wise—apparently by accident. Lady Damerel suddenly appeared at church; having come to Tawton Abbas for three days, to order the distribution of coals, blankets, and Christmas beef—she never omitted those external duties by which many people square accounts with heaven, and keep up a good character on earth. Consequently she always went to church, rain or fair—and this day there fell a heavy storm of December rain. The rector and his wife found her lingering near the chancel door.

"Will you give me shelter for a few minutes?" she asked, in her sweetest and most condescending manner; and Mr. Trevena courteously escorted her under his umbrella to the rectory.

She had seldom been there; only for one or two formal calls; but now she sat down in the little drawing-room as if she meant friendliness rather than formality. After some courteous small-talk about Sir Charles's illness, and the cause of it, chiefly directed to Mr. Trevena—Lady Damerel was always charming to gentlemen—she said carelessly—

"You went away from my garden-party quite early, Mrs. Trevena, before I had time to speak to that tall friend of yours—Mr. —— what was his name? An American, did you say? I rather like Americans."

Susannah was not a coward—her husband sometimes said of her, with his tender jesting, that she "would go up to a cannon's mouth"—if necessary. She felt something like it now. Looking full in Lady Damerel's face, she replied:

"He is not Mr. but Dr. Franklin, a countryman of yours (Sir Charles said you are American)—and a physician in New York."

"Ah! New York. But I am Southern. I was born in Baltimore."

"He said you reminded him of the Baltimore belles," innocently observed the rector. "He thought he had met you somewhere. He is an excellent man. We made acquaintance with him long ago, when traveling abroad; where he once did my wife, and me too, what has turned out to be a great service. Our son, whom of course you know all about, is his godson."

"Oh, indeed," carelessly answered Lady Damerel, with the air of a person not much interested in other people's affairs. "Has your friend gone back to America?"

"He sailed yesterday—Arthur went to Liverpool to see him off."

"How kind! By the way, that son of yours—I must secure him as our accompanist next time I have musical people in the house. He plays extremely well. Is he to be a professional?"

"Oh no!" said the rector with something more than distaste. "He is trying for a scholarship at New College, Oxford, which his Winchester masters think he is sure to get. He is a very clever, as well as a diligent boy."

And the good, unobservant, unreticent, Austin went into details about Arthur's future university career, without noticing the absent smile with which Lady Damerel listened; most people — even parents — are indifferent enough to other people's children.

"Ah, yes—Mr. Arthur's success must be a great pleasure to his father and mother. My children were never clever, nor handsome either, poor little things! Your son is your only one, I conclude? Born late in life, and of course his parents' darling?"

All this while Susannah had sat silently observant—

also, not a little amazed. First, at the extraordinary self-command of the woman, supposing she really was the woman that Dr. Franklin believed her to be; and next, that she should be so ignorant of her neighbors' affairs as never to have heard about Arthur. And yet this was not impossible. In eighteen years the story had died out; people had accepted him so completely as the rector's son—at least in the village; and beyond it the Trevenas knew almost nobody. With a sudden desperate resolve Susannah determined to put Lady Damerel to the test—to tell her the facts, which she must hear ere long, and which it was astonishing she had never heard before. "Tell the truth and shame the devil"—but it was equally to exorcise the devil—that evil spirit which prompted her, the gentle Mrs. Trevena, to fly at Lady Damerel's throat and strangle her.

Looking her full in the face she said distinctly, "I think you do not understand—though it is surprising you should never have heard—that Arthur is not our own son; we have no living children. Dr. Franklin found him for us, and advised us to adopt him. We do not know who were his parents, but he was born at Andermatt, in Switzerland."

Human nature cannot altogether suppress itself. Whatever Lady Damerel had come to seek, she had evidently found something she neither sought nor desired. Her cheek grew ghastly under its paint. She clutched the arm of the chair as if to save herself from falling. Even the unobservant Austin could not help seeing something was amiss, and, courteously observing that the room was very hot, went to open the window.

"Thank you—but I am not ill—only fatigued—worn out with nursing my husband." And then, turning round to Susannah with that mechanical smile which people learn to use in society as well as on the stage, she said—"It is kind of you to give me this confidence. I did not know the boy was not your own. He is—a fine boy—and does you great credit."

And again that ghastly pallor—was it emotion or only fear?—came over her face, till Mr. Trevena offered to fetch her a glass of wine, and looked towards his wife for sympathy and assistance.

But there was no pity—not a jot!—in Susannah's eyes, or in her hard, cold voice.

"Lady Damerel should have ordered her carriage. I am sorry I have no servant here to send. And my son is not at home."

"*My son.*" There was no mistaking the word—or its meaning—its intentional meaning. Lady Damerel removed her hand from her eyes, and the two women steadily regarded one another. In that moment both recognized, without need of words, that each was in possession of the other's secret, and that between them there was war to the knife. All the more deadly because it was a silent war—confined entirely to their two selves. The two mothers between whom King Solomon judged could not hate one another with a more deadly hatred than these—the flesh-and-blood mother who had thrown her blessing away; the real mother who had found it, and kept it—yes, and would keep it, in defiance of the whole world.

Susannah, just and tender woman as she was, could

on occasion be a stern woman too. She had no belief in parental rights, or any rights at all, without their corresponding duties. Years ago she carried off little Nanny, and would have hidden her from her father, separated them entirely, by fair means or foul, until the child was old enough not to be harmed by the man to whom she owed nothing but the mere accident of paternity. What Mrs. Trevena then did—and would have persisted in doing had not fate made it unnecessary —from pure pity, without any personal love for Nanny —would she not be ready now to do for her own Arthur?

Had Lady Damerel confessed all, and begged for the boy—perhaps even then Mrs. Trevena might have had no mercy. She might have said, with Dr. Franklin— "As you made your bed you must lie on it"—and dared the unworthy mother to win one atom of either duty or affection from the son she had cast away. But if any struggle as to the right course was in Susannah's mind, she soon saw it was wholly unnecessary.

"Self-preservation is the first law of nature," says the philosopher; and though sometimes experience has contradicted this—especially in the case of mothers—it exists still.

After a minute or two Lady Damerel rose, her usual stately self, and addressed the rector.

"The rain has abated now, and I must not trouble you any longer. I will walk home, for I never like to use the carriage on Sundays, except for Sir Charles. We think of trying the German spas immediately—so this must be a farewell visit. Make my compliments to your son—I mean your adopted son—and say I congratulate him and his parents."

Evidently the so-called maternal instinct was not in the woman. Whether from conscious guilt or cowardice, she had apparently not the slightest intention of acknowledging her child. A few words of polite adieu, and she had made her escape, having betrayed absolutely nothing.

Susannah was thankful that she too had betrayed nothing—that she had had strength all these months to bear her own burden and trouble no one. The crisis had come, and passed. Now she could breathe again.

Many more weeks and months went by: and untroubled peace. Arthur was at Winchester—Sir Charles and Lady Damerel were traveling abroad. Nothing had happened: and she began to feel that nothing would happen: that she might live and die—dying did not seem so far off at nearly sixty—with her secret unrevealed, keeping Arthur as her son till death.

He seemed more than ever her son, when coming back for summer holidays—triumphant too, for he had gained his scholarship, and was going up to Oxford next term —he found his "dear little mother" a good deal changed. Her pretty brown hair had grown silver-white; her bright cheerfulness—the gayety of sound pure health, though she was never robust—had greatly departed. He could not understand it. She said she was "quite well"—"quite happy"—but she seemed so quiet, so suddenly changed from a middle-aged into an old woman. He wondered nobody saw it—not even her husband.

"Papa," he said, "I think mother wants a little

nursing and companionship. When I am gone to Oxford, suppose you send for Nanny? Let her come a day or two before I leave, and I'll teach her how to take care of mother; only she is such a child still—perhaps she might not understand."

But in spite of Arthur's gentle patronizing, and firm conviction that nobody could take care of his mother except himself—it was found that Nanny did understand; that Miss Grogan had made a little woman of her already, and a capital nurse. Neat, accurate, practical: chary of words, but prompt in deeds; and doing everything necessary without making any unnecessary fuss about it, Nanny, though at first not exactly welcome to her aunt, soon became so, as well as to her uncle. And though still small, dark, and plain, there was a sweetness in her brown eyes, a fairy lightness in her dainty figure, which made her decidedly not ugly. Youth never is ugly, unless it has got an ugly soul.

"She's not so bad, is she, mother?" said Arthur, after the first two days. "She isn't a beauty certainly—she doesn't sweep about the room like Lady Damerel; but I hate tall women!—No woman should ever be bigger than my little mother. Nanny will never be pretty—like you—but she's a nice little thing."

What mother could resist such tender flattery from a big son, not twenty yet, but fully six feet high? What mother could look into that boyish face—knowing the heart was as innocent as the face—and not feel that whatever he said was true, and whatever he did was right?

As for the "nice little thing"—was it surprising that

M

she adored Arthur? as she had done ever since she was a small child; though she had ceased to show it now—at least, not very much—but Mrs. Trevena saw it in her eyes, and sometimes felt a little sorry for Nanny. Still, the child was only a child; and Arthur could not be expected to take much notice of her—such a man as he was grown—and just going up to Oxford. Nor did he notice her at first; being absorbed by his matriculation work.

But all young creatures like one another's company: and when of summer evenings "the children" went off a walk together, leaving Mr. and Mrs. Trevena sitting quietly in the arbor, Susannah said to herself that it was quite natural.

She herself could not take long walks now—nor could she see to read and sew as she once did. She had made over her work-box to the busy useful fingers of Nanny. And instead of reading of evenings, she sat with her hands folded, and thought—we often like thinking as we grow old. Only it is not of ourselves we think; our day is all done—it is of other people.

Strange it was—and yet perhaps not strange—that the last subject which entered Mrs. Trevena's mind should have been that which was most probable, most natural; the story even now beginning to act itself out under her very eyes. The old story, ever new, and which will be new until the end of the world.

She had enacted it herself more than forty years ago, for she was very young when she first met Austin Trevena; and yet it never struck her to think of her boy as anything but a boy, or of Nanny except his small girl-satellite—circling round him with untiring and perfectly natural devotion, but of no importance to him whatever. That one was nearly a man, and the other—alas!—perhaps quite a woman, did not occur to Susannah.

Nor, for a good while, to the young people themselves. Their relations from childhood upwards had been completely "*l'un qui aime, l'autre que se laisse être aimé*"—rather liked it indeed, in an innocent way, for Arthur was neither selfish nor conceited. He had never had a sister, and honestly accepted Nanny as such: teased her, petted her, and took counsel of her by turns: ruled her, yet was led by her—for the little quiet girl had a strong will of her own; and the winning power that many plain-looking but sweet-natured woman have, even over the other sex. And neither he nor any one else suspected that he was gradually slipping into what worldly mothers would call an "entanglement"—but of which the knots are often woven by a kindly Providence to be a man's protection throughout life. Especially such an one as Arthur, who, out of his very simplicity, affectionateness, and lack of personal vanity, was likely to attract every woman he came near.

It was not an ordinary "falling in love"—that headlong tumble which parents and guardians so dread: but a gradual gliding into love; love awaking so early that the young people understood neither its nature nor its name. For instance, the caress begun when, the child's poor mother lying dead in the next room, Susannah had said, "Arthur, kiss Nanny,"—was continued quite naturally, at meetings and partings, until the very day that

Arthur left for Oxford; when his mother noticed, with some momentary surprise, that they merely shook hands. But she soon forgot it—her own heart was so full. And when the little Nanny, who found her wandering forlornly about the empty house—so very empty now Arthur was gone—took her hand and kissed it, Mrs. Trevena embraced her with a burst of feeling, as being the one other person who missed Arthur nearly as much as his mother did.

Shortly afterwards, Nanny was summoned back to Miss Grogan, who was seriously ill, and needed her sorely. Both her uncle and aunt missed her too—a good deal. Likewise at Christmas, when she had promised to return, but did not, and the rectory household had to make the best of the busy time without her. Mr. Trevena distributed his coals and blankets alone; and Arthur wandered aimlessly about the deserted park—for the Damerels were still away. Both father and son openly lamented Nanny, who was "so funny," and "so useful," to which the mother, shut helplessly indoors, agreed with a sympathizing smile, hiding a silent pain that she could be no longer all they required, to either husband or son. But it soon passed—they were both well and strong and happy—and they loved her so much that as long as she sat, even with folded hands, at the fireside, they were sure to think it bright.

After Christmas came a sudden event, ominous of changes—Miss Grogan died. Nanny was left—as she said in her sorrowful letter—"alone in the world." But, as she also said, she meant to face the world, and trouble nobody. She had had a good education—thanks to her uncle, and her dear dead friend; and through all her grief there ran a thread of cheerful courage which touched everybody's heart.

"Nanny is sure to do well," said Mrs. Trevena, affectionately. "Shall we have her here for a while?"

"I wish we could have her here for always," answered the rector.

But, to the surprise of both, Nanny refused their kindness—very gratefully, yet very firmly. She wished to begin to work at once. Nothing would induce her, she said, to eat the bread of idleness. She intended to go out as a governess immediately.

"Impossible!" said her uncle, thinking of her as the last of the Trevenas. "Impossible," wrote Arthur from Oxford, assigning no reason. And "impossible!" added, gravely, Mrs. Trevena, who knew what governess-life is to a girl of eighteen.

But fate—in the shape of Mr. Hardy—Arthur's High Church friend, stepped in and settled the difficulty. He had a widowed sister come to live with him, who would be most thankful to get a daily governess for her only girl. "If Miss Trevena would condescend," he said. "At least so far as to come on a visit to the rectory, and try it for the summer." Miss Trevena, being humble-minded, and strongly urged by both uncle and aunt, did condescend—and came.

She looked so sweet, with her pale face and her deep mourning, that all the curate's family fell in love with her at once; and when Arthur came home for his Easter vacation he found her quite settled: living at the rectory, and walking across the park every day to her work.

It, and what she laughingly called her "parish duties"—as her aunt's substitute—absorbed her so much that, as Arthur openly complained, he saw almost nothing of her, and was left "out in the cold." At which his mother so compassionated him that she took every opportunity of sending him and Nanny for an evening walk together; rejoicing to see them come back merry and happy. Their youthful happiness was the greatest bliss she knew. It helped her to bear her own feebleness and weariness: that shadow of fast-advancing old age—which had come all the faster since the blow of last year.

Do what she would, she could not escape a perpetual fear of "something happening"—some effort on Lady Damerel's part to reclaim her son; or worse, some discovery which might make Arthur's birth not the safe mystery that it now was, but an open disgrace that might wound him to the quick—if a man ought to be wounded by anything in which he himself is entirely innocent.

It was not difficult to divine, or at least to guess at, Lady Damerel's history. The beautiful "public" woman —half a pariah—as it was then thought, though now, thank heaven, many a public and professional woman leads as domestic a life as any private matron who "suckles fools and chronicles small-beer"—married early to a poor gentleman; resenting and hating the restraints of home; heartless, pleasure-loving, though not actually vicious; incapable of love, but too selfish to degrade herself; a "woman of genius," possibly, but with an unwomanly heart; detesting children, and the burden of them; disliking dullness and poverty, and ready always to act on impulse rather than judgment—it was easy to see how all had come about.

Not so easy to see how all would end, or how it ought to end. Sometimes Susannah thought and thought, till she was half dazed—she had come to the time when one must think, for one can do little else; and all one's thoughts are for others—one's own future is of no interest now: but her thoughts all came to nothing, for she could do nothing. Also Dr. Franklin, whose wife had burnt the important letter, wrote advising her to do nothing till he came back to England next year.

So she drifted on, nor noticed how other things and people were drifting on too, unto a future over which she had no jurisdiction and no claim.

That year spring came in early, deliciously;. the tempting spring, when

"A young man's fancy lightly turns to thoughts of love,"

and even old men—at any rate old women—turn half tenderly to memories of what love was, or might have been—when the sight of a face, the touch of a hand, brought unutterable, impossible bliss. Even the rector and his wife, sitting in their lovely garden, with trees budding, primroses blooming, and thrushes singing—felt the nameless charm, and kept their silver wedding-day in tender content: Susannah telling the "children," with a sweet faint blush on her old cheek, how she and papa had met when quite young, and had made a solemn vow among some gooseberry bushes—eating gooseberries plentifully meantime—that they would certainly be married some day; which vow, after half a lifetime, they kept. But she never noticed—nobody noticed—that at her innocent little story Nanny turned very pale, and Arthur very red; and they scarcely spoke to one another for the rest of the day.

It was a rather momentous day, for both inward home pleasure and outside news. Mr. Hardy appeared, in much excitement. His grateful bishop had that day rewarded his long service by an unexpected living; and though now nigh upon forty, the good curate was as happy as a boy. His vicarage was only a few miles off, so he would not lose his friends at the rectory; though, Mrs. Trevena suggested, Nanny would lose her pupil. To which, in some confusion, Mr. Hardy answered that "he was not sure."

Something constrained in his manner—and Nanny's too—startled Mrs. Trevena into remembering how very often he had been at the rectory of late, and how continually he had walked home with Nanny across the park. She smiled to herself, not ill-pleased, for Mr. Hardy was an old friend and an excellent man, young and cheerful for his age. And Nanny, though so much his junior, was such a grave, steady, reliable little thing —just the girl for a country clergyman's wife. She wondered she had never thought of this before—and, woman-like, was thinking it over with unmixed satisfaction, when a name caught her ear—the name which, now she had grown weak and nervous, always seemed to go through her like a knife.

"Have you seen Lady Damerel, Arthur? I met her driving, and she asked me how all was going on at the rectory, and if you and I would come and have an evening of music—quite quietly—they have brought no company down with them. I hear Sir Charles has broken down very much, and cannot live long. Poor Lady Damerel!"

"Poor Lady Damerel, indeed!" echoed Mr. Trevena. "What a change for her! And they say she hates the heir-at-law—a needy man with seven children. What a pity Lady Damerel has none!"

Mr. Hardy agreed, and again asked Arthur to come, as "her ladyship"—he always spoke with much awe of her ladyship—had said she especially wished for him, on account of his music.

"I won't go," said Arthur decidedly. "I don't care for Lady Damerel, though she does sing so well. And why doesn't she invite my mother? I'll not go to Tawton Abbas, or anywhere, without my little mother," added he caressingly.

"But your mother is not able to go, and I think you ought," said the rector, who, like most men, was not indifferent to the charming flattery of Lady Damerel.

Arthur looked at his mother.

"Yes, go," she answered—for a sudden desperation had seized her. Her boy should see with his own eyes, and judge with his own heart, between his natural, unnatural mother, and the woman who had been to him everything that a mother ought to be. "Go," she said, knotting her trembling hands together, and hoping that no one noticed in her the slightest hesitation or pain.

So it came about that during his Easter vacation Arthur went several times to Tawton Abbas, which, notwithstanding Sir Charles's critical state, was full of company—Lady Damerel would not live without it; company among whom a young Oxford man who was handsome and ready-witted, could play and sing, act and dance, with equal facility and enjoyment, was most valuable—and valued. Arther declared it was "capital fun," and took all his "spoiling" with the most frank unconcern, coming home and joking about it to his mother and Nanny. Between the Arcadian life of mornings with Nanny, and the fashionable life of evenings, or rather nights—for he generally came back from Tawton Abbas when all the rectory had gone to bed—the young fellow seemed to be thoroughly enjoying himself—till one day.

Mr. Hardy, after a long walk with Arthur, an interview with Mr. Trevena in the study, and another with Mrs. Trevena in the garden, formally made an offer of marriage to Miss Trevena; he did it in the properest, most orthodox way—indeed the good man's wooing seemed like a bit out of Sir Charles Grandison, only that he proved to be not the "man of men" to his Miss Byron.

Exceedingly agitated, more so than her aunt expected or could account for, the "little girl," now advanced to the dignity of a woman, declared she had never given the slightest encouragement to her suitor, and would certainly not marry him. To all arguments from Mrs. Trevena, and a few very lame ones from Arthur—whom Mr. Hardy had made his confidant, and implored to use his brotherly influence—Nanny answered, pale as death, but with firm composure, that she had made up her mind not to marry anybody, and did not wish another word said on the subject.

So, within a few hours, the thunder-storm came, broke, and passed away: but it left a troubled atmosphere in the happy family. The rector could not get over his startled perplexity at finding his little niece a woman, and Mrs. Trevena knew enough of the cares of governess-ship to regret that Nanny should not escape from them into the blessed haven of domestic life. To her Mr. Hardy seemed very lovable; but evidently Nanny did not love him—and this wise foolish old woman, who still believed in love, had not another word to say.

The storm had passed, but it left its traces behind. Nanny looked dull and sad, and Arthur, who for some reason or other did not "go up" for a few days after term began, was not himself at all.

"Is anything vexing you, my boy?" asked his mother one night when he came in from his usual evening entertainment at Tawton Abbas. He tried to put her off—scolding her for sitting up, and declaring it was because she knew how pretty she looked in her dressing-gown and her picturesque night-cap. But she saw something was amiss, and at last, taking his candle out of his hand, and making him sit down beside her, she found it out.

"That Lady Damerel is an odd woman—a very odd woman," he said. "What do you think she wants me to do? To give up my quiet life at Oxford—I'm obliged to be a reading man, you know, or else I couldn't make ends meet—and go in for a regular jolly life. And she'd give me three hundred a year to do it with. Did you ever hear of such an offer? from a complete stranger too."

"And you answered?"

"I said I was much obliged, of course, but that I had no idea of being a pensioner on any one's bounty. I meant to stand on my own feet and earn my own living as soon as ever I could."

"And she?"

"Oh! she took it coolly enough—as she does everything; said I might please myself, but I had better think it over—only I must speak to no one about it. 'Except my mother,' I said, and then she laughed— Lady Damerel has the most unpleasant laugh I ever heard. I can't like her for all her kindness, and I won't try. And so I won't accept anything from her—not a thing," added Arthur decidedly. "Don't you think I am right, mother?"

"Yes," Susannah said beneath her breath. She was clutching her boy's hand—carressing it and patting it, as she used to do when he was a baby.

"I can't imagine why she should make such a fuss over me. It's bothering—it's humiliating. Can she do it out of compassion? or impertinent patronizing from a grand lady to—— Mother," he added abruptly, "do you think Lady Damerel knows who I am? I mean— does she know I have no right to the name I bear?"

"Everybody knows everything, my darling," said Susannah. "It was the only right, safe, and honorable way. Everybody recognizes you as our dear adopted son, who will be a credit to our name, and make a name for himself besides—as a brave man can."

"And I will. But, mother, sometimes—it's rather hard."

Susannah did not deny. She knew, to the very bottom of her soul, that it was hard.

"If I were a girl now, it wouldn't matter. King Cophetua may woo the beggar-maid; and if she is a queenly maid, and deserves him, it's all right—nobody asks any questions. Poor old Hardy asked none about Nanny. She might never have had a father or a mother for all he cared. He loved her for herself. And he was sure of himself—that he could offer her a good income and an honest name, and creditable relations. Now, if I were to ask a girl to marry me—not that I'm going to, without one halfpenny to rub upon another—but if I were—and her father put the plain question, 'Who are you?' what should I say? It's funny, mother!—but you must allow it's a little hard."

He laughed—not without bitterness—the bitterness that she had long foreseen must come, and wondered it had not come sooner. How could she help him? By telling him the truth, which might be crueller than ignorance? And besides, she herself did not absolutely know the truth—she only guessed at it. If she could have proved it, and thereby given her son name, fortune, every possible worldly prosperity, no matter though she robbed herself of all the joy of her life—still Susannah was the kind of a woman to have done this.

Not now. It might be that Arthur's finding out the truth would take from him what he had, and give him nothing in return—leave him worse than nameless, worse than parentless. She looked up at him as he stood there—pale with a deeper emotion than she had ever yet seen in him, but young, strong, resolute, able to take his destiny in his own hands and carve out his own future—the best thing that can happen to any young man.

"Arthur," she said, "it is hard—in some ways; but if I were you I would not be afraid. What does your favorite poet say?

'For man is man and master of his fate.'

So are you. And sometimes," she spoke bitterly, remembering old days, "it is almost a blessing to have no relations."

"You are thinking of papa and his brother—Nanny's father—whom I hated. He was so cruel to Nanny."

"Yes, but we have forgotten that now. Nanny has not a bit of her father in her, except his name. She is upright, honest, independent—sure to do well in the world. And so will you."

Arthur's eyes brightened. "I will try."

"And remember, my boy—every one has something to fight with—some evil fate to master. I mastered mine, and God gave me you. My dear, isn't it worth a little to you that He also gave you your mother?"

She held out her arms to him; and, big fellow as he was, the boy knelt down, laid his head on her lap, and wept like a child.

That night Susannah made up her mind. Come what might, she would be resolved; she would find out the whole truth. Her son should not be lured from her by temptations of the world, the flesh, and the devil. If he went, he should go open-eyed—choosing deliberately between her and Lady Damerel; the simple, pure, righteous life in which he had been brought up, and the shallow worldly life they led at Tawton Abbas.

So, next day, when the rector and Nanny had gone on their parish rounds together, and Arthur was amissing somewhere—he was often amissing now; being restless, unhappy, weary of his own company, and other people's too—Mrs. Trevena gathered up all her feeble strength, and set out to walk alone across the park to the great house. A short stroll, yet she had not done so much for many months. But the more fast-increasing she felt her weakness, the more she was determined to conquer it, and to work while it was day.

It was a lovely morning; the sky bright with floating white clouds, the trees in the park already growing green. What a beautiful park it was! For nearly twenty years she had watched it, budding with spring, deepening into the full verdure of summer; then melting to the glowing tints of autumn, and the scarcely less lovely whiteness of winter. How she had admired and enjoyed it! much more, probably, than its successive tenants had done. Infinitely more, alas! than its owner, poor Sir Charles! whom she saw coming towards her down the path in his Bath-chair. At first she thought she would avoid him: and then—no!

Sir Charles was such a permanent invalid, such an unconsidered nothing in the Damerel establishment, that Mrs. Trevena had rarely spoken to him. The chair, with its melancholy occupant and the tall footman lounging beside it, was passing her by, when she stopped it—half ashamed of herself to think that it was not for pity she did so. She addressed the old man courteously and kindly, but vainly she tried to get a coherent word from him. He was evidently paralyzed, for his speech was thick, and his face expressionless. His hands, distorted with rheumatism, lay helpless in his lap—yet he must have been a handsome man once. He had sweet soft eyes, blue even yet—as blue as Arthur's; and the clear-cut aquiline features of the Damerels—"a nose as big as mine," she remembered Arthur had once said. Yes, withered and old as it was, the face was Arthur's face—the smile was Arthur's smile. Nature had avenged herself upon the careless wife, the unthankful mother, with circumstantial evidence stronger than any words. Mrs. Trevena saw—and wondered she had never seen it before—that if Sir Charles Damerel and Arthur were set side by side, no one could doubt that the boy was his father's son.

Well, it was good to be assured—whatever might happen; also with a sad pity that removed all conscience-stings as to any claim of the father on the son, she felt that this poor dead-alive wreck of humanity was long past being affected, for good or ill, by anything that did happen. To find a son would be to Sir Charles now neither joy nor pain. It was Lady Damerel only with whom Mrs. Trevena had to do battle; and would do it, putting herself and her feelings entirely aside—as she had had to do all her life; a curious contrast to that other woman, to whom self had been first object always.

It was so still, to judge by the luxury of the morning-room, into which Mrs. Trevena was shown. All looked *couleur de rose*, down to the very hangings, which were so placed as to throw a becoming glow on the faded face of the *passée* beauty who was afraid to be old. Susannah, catching sight of herself in the numerous mirrors, and conscious of her trembling limbs and beating heart, knew that she was old—no doubt about that now! But she grieved not, feared not. All the more reason that she should do what she had to do, without delay.

What was there to do? Nothing, it seemed, by the easy condescending smile with which the great lady received the rector's wife, and the pleasure she expressed at Mrs. Trevena's being able to walk so far, for a mere call.

"It is not a mere call. I wanted to speak to you."

Lady Damerel started an instant—and then resumed her polite smile of attention.

"I am sure anything I can do for you, or for our excellent rector——"

"Thank you—my husband and I want nothing. But you have offered to do something for my son, which he cannot accept—which I do not wish him to accept."

"Why not?"

"Because it is unseemly, and humiliating, for a young man to receive a large annual income from the bounty of—a stranger."

Lady Damerel put her fan before her face, with an air as nonchalant as it was graceful; scarcely to hide emotion: there seemed none to hide.

"I hope that Arthur"—she saw Mrs. Trevena wince—"I beg his pardon, Mr. Arthur, does not consider me quite a stranger. I like the young man; he is useful and pleasant to me—who have no children of my own. If I wish to help him why should you hesitate to accept my offer?"

N

"I do not hesitate," said Susannah; "I absolutely refuse. While I live, my son shall never be indebted for a halfpenny to any one but his mother."

"I thought you told me you were not his own mother?"

"I am not. Are you?"

The question was so sudden—so direct—delivered with the intensity almost of a blow, struck as it were for dear life—that it fell upon Lady Damerel like a blow. She sprang up in her chair.

"What right have you to say this—what proofs can you give?—Mrs. Trevena, how dare you——?"

"I dare do anything, if it is for my son's sake, my boy, whom I took as a little baby—whom I have brought up—who has been all in all to me these twenty years—the best son that ever mother had. How dare *you* come between me and him? How can you, if, as I believe, you are the woman that deserted him, sold him, think to buy him back again with your miserable money? How dare you, I say?"

As Susannah spoke, the passion of her voice startled even herself. But it met no response, either of fear or anger.

Lady Damerel sat down again with a slight laugh. "This is—an amusing fiction. But even if it were the truth——"

"It is the truth, and you know it. And you know that Dr. Franklin knows it too. He will be coming back to England shortly; he and I between us can prove everything—everything. And we will do it."

Lady Damerel smiled still; but in somewhat ghastly

fashion. "That would be unwise, Mrs. Trevena. You would lose your son, and I should not gain mine. One question—does he—the boy—know it too?"

"He does not. If he did, how he would despise you!"

There was no attempt at disguise now. The two women sat looking at one another—open enemies; tiger-like, each ready for the next spring. But both were very quiet; the one through fear, the other from speechless contempt. What would have happened next—who can tell?—but for one of those coincidences which occur sometimes, in a way so natural that we call it providential. As Susannah did, to the end of her days.

The door opened, and Arthur walked in.

"I hope I am punctual, Lady Damerel. You told me to come at eleven. What?"—seeing Mrs. Trevena—"Oh mother, how wrong of you to come alone! How tired you look! Sit down—sit down."

And he stood beside her, with his hand laid caressingly on her shoulder, and his eyes full of anxiety. He had evidently no thought of anybody but his mother. Then, with the intuition of love, he saw that something was the matter; and, with his usual frankness, faced it at once.

"I conclude, Lady Damerel, you know already what I came to tell you—that my mother would rather I did not accept your kindness. I agree with her. I wish to make my own way in the world, owing nothing to anybody—except my mother."

Was it a lingering touch of human nature—maternal

jealousy if not maternal tenderness—that made Lady Damerel's lip quiver as she looked at the handsome, graceful youth, and the little old woman over whom he leant so affectionately.

"Your adopted mother, you mean. But decide as you choose. I hope you may not live to regret it."

Arthur flushed painfully. "Since you know the truth about my birth, Lady Damerel, you will allow that I am right, not only in loving, but in obeying my mother."

As Susannah clung to her boy's hand—the strong young hand which enfolded hers (and here again Nature had asserted herself, for it was the very image of Lady Damerel's)—a sudden revulsion came over her. She felt compelled by that sense of absolute right, quite irrespective of worldly wisdom or personal feeling, that stern law—"Fais ce que tu dois, advienne que pourra!" which strengthens some people—women especially—to do by impulse that which in cold blood they would perhaps have shrunk from doing.

"Thank you, my own good boy!" she said, with a sob. "You know how I have loved you. But I am not your mother. Your real mother—the woman who bore you—is—that woman there!"

Arthur sprang up as if he had been shot. "She my mother! the mother who deserted me—sold me?—oh no, mother darling! it can't be true—it isn't true!"

"It is true. She does not deny it. Look at her."

Lady Damerel sat bolt upright in her chair—as white and as hard as marble. Arthur took one step towards her, and then drew back.

"Thank you, mother, for telling me. I am glad I know this. It was right I should be told."

"I did not wish him to be told. No good can come of it, for his father never knew of his existence. I shall be glad to help him—with the half of my fortune if he wishes—after Sir Charles's death. But I never can acknowledge him publicly. It would ruin me."

Lady Damerel spoke in a slow, cold, impersonal voice, never looking at her son. Nor did her son look at her. Rather he turned away his eyes, as if the mere sight of her were painful to him. At last he said, very quietly —and with a strange absence of emotion which made him for the moment almost resemble her—

"You need not fear: I shall never intrude upon you. I think it would almost kill me to have to do my duty to you as your son. Good-morning, Lady Damerel. Come, mother, let us go home."

He placed Mrs. Trevena's hand within his arm, and, with a distant, stately bow—a bow worthy of the heir of all the Damerels—he quitted without another word "the woman that bore him"—who had been to him merely that and nothing more.

Lady Damerel sat, in her unshared splendor, childless and alone. Her sin *had* found her out. It was a just and a righteous retribution.

CHAPTER VIII.

For several days after Arthur discovered the truth about his parentage, he and his "mother" never spoke on the subject. He had whispered to her on their way home from Tawton Abbas—" Please don't say a word to me—I can't bear it"—and indeed she was utterly unable to say a word. The long strain being ended, a reaction came. Ere nightfall she was so ill that Arthur silently put off his departure for Oxford; and for many days neither he nor any one at the rectory thought of aught but her—the centre of all their love and care.

When she revived, she found that Arthur had told both the rector and Nanny what had happened—the bare fact—no more—" to save mother the pain of telling it" —but that he had requested of them total silence on the subject, since this discovery "made no difference in anything."

He repeated the same to herself in the few words that passed between them before he started for Oxford: she had thought it right to speak, and explain to him that even though he were the lawful heir of Tawton Abbas, unless Lady Damerel acknowledged this, it would be most difficult to prove his rights.

"It does not matter, mother," he said calmly. "I

have thought it all over, and perhaps "'Tis better as it is'—as your friend Shakspere says. I will make my own way in the world, and be indebted to nobody. Except you—except you!"

He stooped and kissed the silver hair—whiter even within the last few weeks. Then, holding his head high, though he too looked older and graver—much, he bade her and them all a cheerful good-bye, and went back to his work.

From that time Arthur's letters came regularly, even more regularly than usual. But they were only to his mother—not to Nanny, who had once shared them. And they were wholly about his work—or his play, for he was equally good at both; as noted on the river as he was in the schools. But he never in the least alluded to what had occurred, or implied that he himself was in any way different from the Arthur Trevena who had been the Trevenas' only son, dearly beloved, for the last twenty years.

And Lady Damerel made no sign. She still stayed on at Tawton Abbas—which, it was clear, poor Sir Charles was never likely to leave again; but she filled it with company, as usual, and lived her usual lively life there. Her sole appearance in the village was at church, where she sat, erect as ever, in her arm-chair; her cold, handsome, painted face, under the thin gauze veil which she always wore, contrasting strangely with the background of marble monuments—the old Damerels to whom her husband would soon be gathered. Sir Charles, it was rumored, would be the last of the name, though not of the race; for the next heir being by the female line, the baronetcy would become extinct. Though she was little known, and less liked, one or two of the more thoughtful of the congregation, looking at her, and recognizing what a downcome must follow her husband's death, sometimes said—" Poor Lady Damerel!"

Not Mrs. Trevena. Under all her gentleness Susannah could, if need required, be as hard as stone, and as silent. She never, in or out of the house, except upon compulsion, mentioned the name of Lady Damerel. She rose up from her illness, and went about her duties as heretofore—not even allowing Nanny to share them; Nanny, who still lived at the rectory, nominally, but was rarely at home, having obtained teaching in a neighboring town. She was cheerfully earning her honest bread, and evidently making up her mind to do this all her days, as if there had been no such person as Mr. Hardy in existence. She worked hard, poor little thing!—as her aunt had done before her; and her aunt appreciated this, as well as the tenderness which made Nanny, whenever she was at home, as good as any daughter.

But Susannah did not want a daughter. All her heart was bound up in her son; and it was a great pang to her, even though she acknowledged it might be "all for the best"—when Arthur announced his intention of spending the long vacation with a reading party in Wales. He could afford it, having earned some extra money by accidental "coaching." It was good for his health, his mother argued to herself; and would be more cheerful to him than home—which he must find rather dull now he was a grown-up young man. So she said to Nanny, who listened and said nothing; Nanny never did speak much at any time.

Therefore it befell that for a whole year Arthur appeared at the rectory only on very short visits; between terms, or after having passed successfully all his examinations. He would never "set the Thames on fire"—as he one day bade Nanny impress upon his mother; but he had no fears of failing in his university career. Indeed he hoped to get through it in such a way as to secure afterwards his daily bread, at least, probably as an Oxford "coach." Of music, or the musical career, he now never spoke a word.

Indeed, in many ways the boy was much changed—a boy no longer, but a man. In one thing, however, there was no change, but rather a growth—his tender devotion to his mother. Ay, even though life, which with him was pouring on towards flood-tide, with her was at its quiet ebb. Though she could not share in his pleasures, could never be to him the sympathetic companion that young and active mothers often are to their boys—and a lovely sight it is!—still, to see Arthur with his little old mother, as careful as a girl, as devoted as a lover, as tender as a son—was also a sight never to be forgotten.

Lady Damerel never saw it—nor they her. Once, when walking in the park, they came across Sir Charles's wheeled chair; Arthur, taking off his hat, stood aside to let it pass, with its melancholy occupant, behind whom walked the valet, or keeper, always his sole companion.

"It is no use speaking to Sir Charles; he doesn't know anybody now," said the servant carelessly; and they walked on. But, in the blank white face of the old man, and the strongly-marked profile of the young one,

Susannah saw again that unmistakable likeness—fate's confirmatory evidence against the cruel bar-sinister which the world would be sure to impute to a deserted child. And though to judge a man by this, to lay to his charge his parents' sin, is wholly unjust and unchristian; still, since the world is neither christianized nor just, it will be always so.

She watched her boy as he walked on beside her, with a grave fixed look on his face, but showing no other emotion.

"Sir Charles will not live long," she said, "and nobody could wish it."

"No; but I am glad to remember he was always kind to me."

This was all. Intercourse between Tawton Abbas and the rectory had now stopped entirely. The rector wished it to be so. Austin Trevena did not often take the law into his own hands. His own instincts had been so pure, and his life so blameless, that he did not understand sinners, and was apt to be only too lenient to them. But in this case he was very firm.

"The church-door is open to any one," he said, "and I cannot refuse her the sacrament, for I know nothing against her moral character—but there it ends. I hope, Susannah, that Lady Damerel will never darken our doors again."

She did not. For a whole year no trouble entered those quiet doors; where old age was now beginning to claim its Sabbath of peace, which ought to be so welcome and so blessed. For what energetic action is to youth, so is mere rest to declining years. After sixty—sometimes, alas! before then—we learn to say, "There is no joy but calm;"—and to be thankful for it if we get it.

So, when month after month slid by, and nothing happened, nothing broke the monotony of the peaceful household, except Arthur's flying visits, and his constant, comfortable letters—Susannah's worn face gradually recovered its look of sweet content, justifying her boy in telling her, as he did sometimes, that she was "the prettiest old lady that ever was seen." Or would be, one day—for he refused to allow that she was "old" yet; and often proposed the most unheard-of feats for her in the way of picnics, and other expeditions with himself and Nanny. At which she smilingly shook her head, and sent "the children" away by themselves.

Arthur, come home now for the long vacation, seemed again his merry boyish self. He had got triumphantly through his "schools"—and seemed determined to enjoy himself. He went singing about the house as when he was ten years old; though now just past one-and-twenty; he walked, he fished, he bicycled; he "tramped" the parish for the rector, and visited the old women with Nanny, who was also at home for her holidays.

Nanny had changed very little within the last few years. She was still the same plain little thing, except for her great dark eyes, and her exceedingly sweet-toned voice—a pleasant voice is better to live with than even a pretty face. But she had an atmosphere of prettiness about her too—exceeding neatness of dress, and grace of movement; so that, though not a beauty, she could never be called decidedly ugly. Some day, perhaps, some other man—probably, her aunt thought, an elderly man—might find in her the same nameless charm that Mr. Hardy had done. Poor Mr. Hardy! He still came to the rectory sometimes, but he never said a word more to Miss Trevena. Once, when talking to Arthur about the future of "poor little Nanny," his mother suggested that perhaps she might be an old maid after all. At which the boy laughed—which Susannah thought rather un-brotherly and unkind—but he made her no answer whatever.

It was August, and he had been two weeks at home; going about everywhere, except in the direction of Tawton Abbas. It was emptied of guests at last, they heard; for Sir Charles was slowly dying. Lady Damerel seldom appeared at church now; but one day a stranger gentleman was seen there, in the Damerel pew. He was stout, pompous, and common-looking. Report said he was the heir, come to pay a duty visit, and investigate the state of affairs; which made the village talk him over rather curiously, and say again—"Poor Lady Damerel!"

But nobody ever said "Poor Mrs. Trevena!" There was little need. Though feeble and elderly now, she looked so content and at rest—so proud even, when walking into church on her tall son's arm—that no one would ever have thought of pitying her. Nor did she pity herself. Her life's storms seemed to have sunk into peace. Her boy knew everything about himself; and yet was satisfied to be still her boy. Accounts reached her on all sides of his well-doing at Oxford; where, his university curriculum being gone through, a fellowship, and possibly a tutorship, were almost sure to follow;

one of the many proofs that a boy with a fair amount of brains, and the determination to use them, can make his way in the world without any extraneous help, either of friends or fortune—if he so choose. "Where there's a will there's a way," Arthur used to say, as a boy; and as a man he bade fair to carry out his creed.

His mother thought of him now with that restfulness of perfect trust, not so much in his fortunes as in himself—a safer stronghold—which, God help them! not all mothers have, or deserve to have. But He had given her that blessing, and she was thankful. No doubt, Arthur was not quite as perfect as she thought him; but he was a very good fellow, and a favorite with everybody—including all the young ladies of the neighborhood. For he and Nanny together had gradually brought young life about the rectory; where there were occasionally garden-parties, lawn-tennis meetings, and such-like mild country amusements. Susannah shared them, and was amused by them; sometimes speculating upon how much her boy was admired, and wondering who would fall in love with him; and who, in some far future day, he would fall in love with himself, and marry. She would be very fond of his wife, she thought; and oh! it would be delightful to see his children.

"Only fancy! me a grandmother!" she thought, and laughed to herself at the oddness of the idea.

She was sitting, after one of these parties, in the warm August darkness, lit with stars, and fragrant with delicious scents. It was about nine o'clock; Arthur and Nanny had walked a little way down the road with their friends, and the rector was in his study. Susannah sat in the summer-house, all alone. But she did not mind solitude; she rather enjoyed it. She liked to sit and think—as now; for the scent of clematis and jasmine always brought back the August nights of her youth—when Austin came back from Oxford, and they used to walk in his father's garden together for hours. Then, life was all before them; now it was behind. What matter? It had not been all she expected; a ship or two had gone down, but much had been saved—enough to make the old scents always sweet to her, and the old days dear.

She was looking back upon them, dreamily; and forward, into the days to come—not so many now!—when she heard steps upon the gravel, and there passed two figures—a man and a girl. She thought at first it was her house-maid, who she knew had a "lad"—for the man's arm was round the girl's waist, and she was sobbing on his shoulder; which kept Mrs. Trevena from speaking to them. Shortly they passed again, and then, to her utter bewilderment, she saw it was Arthur and Nanny—whom she still sometimes called—"the children."

She was so accustomed to think of them as such, that at first her only feeling was a slight vexation that Nanny should be "bothering" Arthur with her troubles. She had heard him say, "Don't cry, poor little Nanny—please don't." But Nanny was a little too old to be soothed and caressed like a baby, and should be careful as to how such caresses looked outside—Arthur not being her real brother. As to anything else, Mrs. Trevena dismissed the idea as simply ridiculous. Her

Arthur—such a fine young fellow, everybody's favorite; and Nanny—such an ordinary little creature—whom he had played with, petted, tyrannized over all his life—for them to be anything but brother and sister was perfect nonsense! She would not speak to Arthur, or put such a notion into his head; but she would speak to Nanny, who was a sensible girl, and would understand.

However, when she went in-doors, she found Nanny had gone to bed; "very tired," Arthur explained; and that he himself, after supper and prayers, was evidently waiting for a talk with his mother—as he often did of Saturday nights when the rector was busy over his sermon.

"I have rather a serious word or two to say to you, mother darling," he whispered, as he took her hand and sat down beside her.

"Not very serious," smiled she—for his eyes were shining and his manner cheerful and happy, though a trifle nervous. At which she hardly wondered, when he came out suddenly with a startling idea.

"Mother, I want to leave you for a little. I am thinking of going to Switzerland—to Andermatt."

"To Andermatt? Why? Oh, my boy, what good would it do?"

Arthur soothed her momentary distress—he had unlimited power of soothing his mother; and then told her that in consequence of a letter from his godfather, "and for other reasons," he had lately thought it advisable to tell his whole history to a friend he had, the son of an eminent London barrister—who had taken counsel's opinion. This was, that if he ever meant to claim the estate and the baronetcy, he ought immediately to take steps to obtain what is called "perpetuation of testimony," that is, the affidavits of all those witnesses who could prove his birth and his identity; which evidence could be laid up, and would be sufficient, in case of the death of any of them before the time came for the heir to assert his rights.

"I will never do this in Sir Charles's lifetime; but afterwards, I may, if I can afford the money. One's birthright is one's birthright, and worth fighting for. No man could be expected not to fight, if he has the right on his side, both for his own sake and those belonging to him."

"But that is only papa and me; and we would rather keep you as our son than have you the heir of all the Damerels."

No sooner had she said this than she felt how selfish it was, and how natural, how right, that Arthur should feel as he did, and should have done what he had done —as any young man would have done—though it hurt her a little that he had done it without consulting her. But he was so tender, so thoughtful, and withal so prudent, that the feeling soon passed. If her son did what was right and wise, it mattered little whether he did it with her or without her.

So they went into the details of his proposed journey with their usual mutual confidence. He had saved enough to defray all expenses, he thought, if he traveled very economically; and when she offered him money, he refused it. He preferred being "on his own hook."

"You see, I am not doing badly, mother, for a fellow

of twenty-one. It's odd—but I am really twenty-one now. I could be sued for my own debts—or for breach of promise, if I had asked any one to marry me."

He said this with a laugh and a blush—but also with an anxious look out of the corners of his bright honest eyes. His mother laughed too, in unsuspicious content.

"All in good time, my dear. I hope you will marry some day, when you find anybody you care for—which you have not found yet, you know."

Arthur looked grave and answered, very gently, "I am not sure."

A sudden wild apprehension flitted across the mother's mind. Could her boy have fallen in love? The girls of the neighborhood—she counted them over swift as thought. Not one seemed possible, probable, or desirable. "Arthur?" she cried, in an almost agonized question.

Arthur hung his head a little. "Yes, mother, it's quite true. I did really ask her—this evening. I think I must have loved her all my life—though I didn't find it out till Mr. Hardy wanted her, and couldn't get her."

"Nanny! Oh Arthur, it isn't surely Nanny! Impossible!"

"Why impossible?" said Arthur, drawing himself up.

"Such a——" "such a plain little thing," the mother was going to say, but stopped herself—" a different kind of person from you. And she has been your cousin—almost your sister—ever since you were children together."

"But she is not my cousin, and not my sister, and I don't want her as either. I want her for my wife."
O

The young man—he was a man now—spoke firmly the strange new word. It went through his mother like a shaft of steel—yet she had the sense not to show it.

"You asked Nanny, you say, this evening? And she answered——"

"She would not give me any answer at all till I had told you—and her uncle. But I think, indeed I know——" And Arthur lifted his head prouder than ever—with the honest pride of a young man who knows that the girl he loves loves him. "She is such a good girl," he added. "Nobody in the world could ever say a word against my little Nanny."

"*My*" little Nanny! the sense of possession—the passionate protection of his own against all the world—it touched the mother in spite of herself. So many lovers are such cowards—so ardent to seize, so feeble to defend. Here was the true chivalric lover, who, it was clear, meant to hold to his "little Nanny" through thick and thin.

What could Susannah say? It was the very kind of love she most admired—the ideal of faithful tenderness which she herself had taught him; though it broke her heart she could not but respect it. And yet—and yet—

Arthur saw her evident distress, but did not attempt to console her. There is a time—God forgive them, poor lambs!—when all young people think of themselves only. Happy for them if their elders have self-control enough to recognize this—to remember the time when they also went through the same phase of passionate egotism—or dual egotism. It cannot last long. If lovers are proverbially selfish, except to the object beloved, husbands and wives, fathers and mothers, must inevitably soon learn that self-abnegation which is the very soul of marriage and parenthood, which often makes even the most thoughtless boy or girl into a noble man and woman.

There is much to be said for and against what the worldly-minded call "calf-love." It may not always endure—perhaps best not—for a man's last love is sometimes deeper than his first. But sometimes it does endure; and then it is the strongest thing in life; I have known people who loved one another in their teens, and loved on for sixty years.

By a sort of inspiration, Susannah's mind leaped at this truth, or at least this possibility; and it strengthened her to bear what to no mother can be a joy, and may be a sharp pang—the discovery that she has ceased to be her child's first object—that another, perhaps a total stranger, has suddenly become far closer, far dearer, far more important than she.

Restraining a sob, and compelling herself into something like a smile, Mrs. Trevena held out both her hands to her boy. He seized them, and, flinging himself on his knees before her, put both his arms round her waist and kissed her again and again.

"My good mother—my kind mother!" was all he could say, almost with a sob.

She stroked his hair, and patted his shoulder.

"You silly boy—such a mere boy still! And she such a baby—little Nanny, whom you have known all your life."

"It is because I have known her all my life—because I am quite sure of her, that I love her so. She would never despise me. She is willing to marry a man without a name—and therefore for her sake I will try to get one. I'll do nothing just yet—as I told you; I will stand on my own feet and make myself respected as I am. But, by and by, I will move heaven and earth to obtain my own. For Nanny's sake—for Nanny's sake! And, if I fail, I shall still have her—and you."

"Her" first—"you" afterwards. Well! it was right—it was natural; the law of nature and of God. Arthur was unconscious of having said it—nor did his mother betray that she had heard it. It was the final love-sacrifice which all mothers must make; if the smoke of it ascends to heaven, God accepts it, and that is enough.

"You are not vexed—not angry with me, mother darling?" said Arthur anxiously.

"How could I be? You are a couple of little geese—that is all. And you will probably have to wait for years and years."

"Never mind," laughed Arthur, now quite happy—actually radiant in his happiness—so handsome, so graceful, that more than ever it was an actual amazement to her how he, her King Arthur, the cynosure of all eyes—the sort of *preux chevalier* whom most girls fall in love with—he, who might have chosen anybody, should have gone and chosen Nanny—poor little Nanny!

"You will speak to her?" pleaded he. "She is gone to bed, but she is not asleep, I am sure. You will not wait till morning—you'll go now, mother?"

"Certainly." And Mrs. Trevena rose, steadying herself by the back of her chair—and feeling blindly for the door handle. Then she turned. "I think, dear, we'll not tell papa of this just yet—not till after Sunday."

When they did tell him Mr. Trevena was, as his wife had foreboded, a little vexed. He took the masculine and worldly view of the subject, and did not like being disturbed out of the even tenor of his way by any such youthful nonsense.

"Foolish children!—they have not a halfpenny between them," said he. "And the idea that at their age they should know their own minds—it's ridiculous!"

"We did," said Susannah softly. And she may surely be forgiven if, looking at the Austin Trevena of to-day, she remembered the Austin Trevena of forty years ago, and thought perhaps it might have been better for both had he too been "young and foolish"—if they had trusted themselves and Providence; married as early as prudence would allow, spent the flower of their days together, not apart; fought through their cares and enjoyed their blessings; and lived to "see their children's children and peace upon Israel." Such might be the lot of Arthur and Nanny—and, remembering her own lot, she was glad of it.

"Husband," she said, and put her arm on his shoulder with the love that had never failed him all his life—never would fail him till death—"we did not make this marriage—it made itself, or God made it—who knows? Don't you think we had better leave things alone, and let the young people settle their own affairs?

A sentiment which coincided so much with the rector's dreamy, lazy ways that possibly he was glad in his heart to leave things alone. He told his niece "she could do as she liked," and Arthur too; went back to his books and forgot all about it. In his gentle undemonstrative way Austin was the tenderest of husbands—the kindest of men; but with him, as was not unnatural, the days of romance were all over and done.

Were they with Susannah? are they ever with any real woman who recognizes that love is the heart of life; and, for either man or woman, its utmost salvation, its most perfect joy?

Arthur had only a few days at home before he started for Andermatt with his friend, who was also a lawyer, and capable of transacting the necessary legal business. The boy arranged all with the cleverness, shrewdness, and firmness of a man. Between whiles he went about, also like a man, with the girl he had chosen; beamingly happy, and not a bit shy or ashamed. His mother watched him with a full heart—she also "had been in Arcadia."

But it was a sore heart too. She had always liked Nanny, and been very kind to her; but kindness and liking are not necessarily love. People of wide sympathies and active benevolence are often misconceived, and supposed to love everybody. They do not. They feel kindly to everybody, but they only love one or two people in the whole course of their lives. It is like a man putting all his money in one bank;—if the bank breaks—and it does break sometimes—God help him! He may carry on business very successfully outside, but at heart he is bankrupt all his days.

One of these rare loves—strong as rare—in Mrs. Trevena's life, had been the maternal passion for her adopted son. His going to school and college had made him less a part of her daily existence than if he had been a girl; but his falling in love was a greater blow to her than any daughter's would have been. In spite of the cruel jocularities against mothers-in-law, many a woman inclines tenderly to the man her daughter marries; often loving him like her own son. For "her daughter's her daughter all her life"—and she gains a son besides. But when her son marries she loses him in degree, and sometimes does not gain a daughter.

Watching Nanny, and wondering more and more how Arthur ever came to choose her—yet plain little women have ruled paramount, and for life, in the hearts of clever and handsome men—Susannah sometimes felt as if she could never love the girl: and then again as if she must love her, because Arthur did. It was a desperate struggle—a small "tragedy in a tea-pot"—but none the less a tragedy; and all the more pathetic that it went on in the silent heart of an old woman, in whom age, which deadens most things, had never yet deadened the power of loving and of suffering.

But it could not last—it ought not to last. Best to bury it—and let all the sweet charities of life grow up round it, like grass and flowers round a stone.

The houshold at the rectory soon found out the truth of things: so did the village, and came with its innocent congratulations to Mr. Arthur and Miss Nanny. Mr. Hardy came too—sad, but resigned—saying with comical pathos, "It's not lost that a friend gets." By and by all the neighborhood brought good wishes too, except Tawton Abbas, where Sir Charles still lay in that lingering death in life which might last for months or years.

Susannah herself expected little result from Arthur's journey to Andermatt; but she thought it right he should go; and his godfather, who expected to be in England shortly, wrote, insisting on the same. Nanny said nothing—all she cared for was Arthur himself. Her absorbing and exclusive devotion to him, which had evidently existed hopeless for years, touched his mother's heart more than anything else; and made a little easier that salutary but rather melancholy performance of "playing second fiddle," which all parents must learn, soon or late. It is the law of nature—and therefore the law of God.

Mr. Trevena was the only person in the household who dwelt much on the worldly phase of the matter; thought it possible that Arthur might one day be Sir Arthur Damerel, and suggested that the last of the Trevenas would prove a not unsuitable Lady Damerel.

"And then, my dear, you and I must make up our minds to spend our old age together. The common lot! When the young birds are flown we must snuggle down in the empty nest. I dare say we shall bear it."

"Oh yes—we shall bear it," smiled Susannah, as she kissed him tenderly—the one man she had loved all her life through. She knew all his weaknesses—all his faults, as he knew hers; still he was himself, and she was herself—nothing could divide them but death. There is a sentence—if to quote it be not profane—and yet how can it be so, to those who try in all things to imitate the Divine Master? "Having loved his own, he loved them unto the end." And in all true loves we do love—we cannot choose but love—unto the end.

Arthur wrote from Andermatt that he had "found all he hoped for, and done all he wanted to do." Nothing more. Explanations could wait. He and his companion meant to "have their fling," for a week or two; it might be many years before he could afford more foreign traveling, and then he would come home. Home to the brightest and best bit of a young man's life, or a girl's either—when their lot is all settled, their love openly acknowledged; and they start, a betrothed pair, with everybody's good wishes, to begin the journey of life together.

"My dear," said Mrs. Trevena to Nanny, as they sat at their sewing, though the younger did it chiefly now, for Susannah's eyes were fast failing her—"My dear, what day is Arther coming home?" It was a new thing, a rather sore thing, for the mother to have to ask anybody else "when Arthur was coming home?" but the reward, to a generous heart, was Nanny's bright up-look, and happy blush.

"I think, aunt, he will be here the day after to-morrow. But I told him he was not to come till he had done all he wanted to do, and seen everything he wanted to see."

This proud maidenly possession of a man, not to queen it over him in selfish vanity, but to use her influence nobly, for his good and hers—it was a pretty thing to see; and it comforted the mother's heart. She knew well that a man's whole future often depends upon the sort of girl he falls in love with in his first youth.

"I agree with you, my dear; still, if you write again, tell him I think he should come home at once. His godfather is in England, and will be here to-day. You remember Dr. Franklin?"

"Oh yes." There was nothing connected with Arthur which Nanny did not remember. Hers was the most entire, absorbing devotion, reasonable, not blind devotion, that any girl could give; and day by day it was reconciling Arthur's mother to things as they were—even though they were wholly contrary to what she had expected or desired. She could not withstand the pathetic appeal of Nanny's dark eyes—like that of Helena to the Countess, in *All's well that ends well*.

> "Let not your hate encounter with my love
> For loving where you do."

Also, another thing reconciled her—a thing hard to learn, but when learnt, bringing with it a solemn peace. Dearly as she loved her own, she felt she could take care of them no more. As she watched Nanny flitting about like a little brown bird, carrying out her orders, suggesting things she had forgotten, and doing everything she was unable to do, the wife and mother learnt to say to herself, "So be it!"

When Dr. Franklin arrived she made Nanny explain to him the position of Arthur's business affairs; which the girl did so clearly and well that the old man—he was quite an old man now—patted her on the shoulder approvingly.

"My godson has fallen on his feet, whether he ever is Sir Arthur or not. When you write, tell him I say so."

But fortunately there was no need of writing. Next

day Arthur came home, and Dr. Franklin's evidence, conclusive as to identity, and including Lady Damerel's own admission that the child was hers and her husband's, was formally taken.

"Depend upon it, if she finds out I'm here, she'll shake in her shoes," said the Kentuckian, laughing his silent laugh. And truly, when the same evening, the Tawton Abbas carriage passed him, as he stood leaning on the rectory gate, the face that looked out from it turned deadly pale. But Lady Damerel made no sign of recognition. On both sides there seemed an armed truce, to last as long as fate would permit—which could not be very long after all.

Nor was it. Two days after, when the young people, shy, but proud, and unspeakably happy, had slipped away for their daily walk together, leaving Dr. Franklin and Mrs. Trevena sitting in the garden, and the rector in his study—there came a message from Tawton Abbas. The church bell suddenly began to toll, as it had tolled for centuries on the death of any Damerel—once every minute for every year of age. They counted seventy-three strokes. It was Sir Charles Damerel then who had gone to his rest.

All met on the doorsteps of the rectory, listening. Arthur removed his hat, and stood bareheaded, with a grave, composed air, till the bell ceased—then, taking Nanny's hand, led the way indoors. They all followed, for they knew the crisis was come.

A long consultation followed. "Le roi est mort—vive le roi!" There could be no doubt that the heir-presumptive would immediately claim his rights, and that the heir-apparent must claim his, or else for ever hold his peace.

There were two ways of procedure: one was that, supposing the remote cousin appeared at the funeral, having already taken possession, to bring an action of ejectment against him in behalf of the direct heir: the second, involving greater difficulties, was, that Arthur should take possession of Tawton Abbas, and leave his opponent to bring the action of ejectment. But this could not be done without the consent and assistance of Lady Damerel, which would be equivalent to a public acknowledgment of her son.

It was decided to adopt the former course. "If I have to fight—fight I will," said Arthur, with a quiet resolution that surprised everybody. "But I will not do it untenderly. She shall not be troubled in any way till after the funeral."

This was fixed for an earlier day than the village expected. Usually the Damerels had the special honor of remaining above ground for a week or more, before being left to sleep with their fathers under Tawton church. That poor Sir Charles should be buried on the third day, looked far too unceremonious—almost as if his widow were glad to get rid of him. And when it was noised abroad that the heir was "somewhere on the continent," taking one of his numerous sons to school in Germany, and that consequently Lady Damerel would be the only chief mourner, everybody was still more astonished.

Except Dr. Franklin. "That woman's a shrewd one," he said. "She knows on which side her bread's buttered. I shouldn't wonder——"

And there he stopped. Nobody talked very much at the rectory, except on commonplace, extraneous subjects, during those three anxious days.

The funeral day was a cheerless one, such as comes sometimes in September; a settled downpour, when it appears as if the weather has broken, and the summer is gone. Nevertheless half the neighborhood assembled in the chilly church—so damp and cold that Nanny entreated her aunt not to attempt to go; and carriage after carriage rolled past the rectory gate on its way to pay respect to the last of the Damerels. It was to be a very fine funeral, everybody agreed; Lady Damerel having spared no expense to make her sorrow for her husband as public as possible.

The long procession had been already seen wending along the park, and the rector was putting on his canonicals, when Arthur came into the study, dressed in complete mourning.

"My boy?" said Mrs. Trevena questioningly. She only questioned now—she never controlled: he had a right to judge and act for himself; and she knew he would do both rightly.

He stooped and kissed her tenderly. "You do not object? I am going to my father's funeral." It was the first time he had ever used the word: he said it now with a lingering pathos, as we speak of something wholly lost—the loss of which teaches us what it might have been. "I ought to go, I think. He was a good man. There is one thing I shall find it hard to forgive; that I was prevented—she prevented me—from ever knowing my father."

"But that gained you a mother, young fellow!" said Dr. Franklin sharply. "You've won much more than you lost."

"I know it," said Arthur earnestly. "And if all fails, I shall come home here, and then go to Oxford and earn my honest bread, with Nanny beside me." It was Nanny's hand he took—Nanny's eyes he looked into when he spoke. Then, as with a sudden thought, he added—"But I shall be my mother's son all my days."

Again he kissed her, and his mother kissed him back again; nor hindered him, nor grieved him, by a single look or word.

They all went to the church together, for Mrs. Trevena refused to be left behind. Arthur did not enter the rectory pew with the rest, but stood at the entrance, waiting till the body was borne in to those solemn sentences which all of us know sadly well, beginning—"Man that is born of a woman."

After it walked Lady Damerel, in her widow's weeds; erect and steady, but alone—in that utmost heart-loneliness which a woman, if she has a heart at all, can feel, when husband and children have gone to the grave before her, and she only is left, to a desolate old age. As she passed him, she looked up and saw Arthur. He did not look at her—his eyes were fixed on the coffin: but at some slight gesture she made he stepped forward—as he might have intended to do in any case—and took his place beside her.

The service continued. The body was lowered into the vault—the solemn spadeful of "earth to earth" rattled down—heard distinctly through the dark, chilly church;—there was the final pause—the last gaze into that gloomy cave of death—and Lady Damerel turned to go.

"She's fainting," Arthur heard somebody whisper. Whether she took the help, or he offered it, he never knew; but her hand was upon his arm, and leaning heavily, almost staggering sometimes, she passed through the respectful if not very sympathetic crowd, to the church door. There, almost in her path, stood the gaunt figure of the Kentucky doctor; who knew—had known —everything.

Perhaps the woman felt that all was over, and determined to do with a good grace what she would soon be compelled to do; which after all might be the best and most prudent thing for her to do. Or—may be— let us give her the benefit of the doubt—even thus late, nature was tugging at her heart. When Arthur had put her into the carriage, and was lifting his hat with a formal farewell bow, she leant forward and seized his hand.

"Come home with me! You must—it is necessary. I will confess;—you shall claim your rights—everything will be yours."

The boy hesitated a moment—he was a man and yet a boy; he turned very pale, and looked round—was it for his real mother? who was not the woman that bore him. But Dr. Franklin behind said imperatively "Go!"— and he went.

What the two said to one another when shut up in the carriage together, or what revelations were made that afternoon, when Dr. Franklin, having been sent for by the family lawyer, who of course had come for the funeral, went up to Tawton Abbas, was never clearly explained, but before nightfall the news had run like wildfire through the village that Arthur Trevena, the rector's adopted son, had been suddenly discovered to be Sir Arthur Damerel, Sir Charles's lawful heir. Of course a large amount of fiction was mingled with fact. The presumptive heir—the second cousin once removed—arrived post-haste next day—just too late for the hasty funeral—(she was a clever woman, Lady Damerel!)—and it was said he intended to fight it out by law. However, either he became convinced that litigation was hopeless; or had no money to waste among lawyers; he swallowed his disappointment and stayed on placidly at Tawton Abbas. He even, some weeks after, assisted cheerfully at the ringing of bells, the roasting of oxen, and other festivities—which indicated the delight of the neighborhood that "poor Sir Charles" was not the last of the Damerels.

The strange story was a nine days' wonder; and then it all died out. It was nobody's business except the Damerels'; and they were satisfied. The widow—who had been seen by nobody except the lawyers—went away "for change of air," and Sir Arthur Damerel reigned in his father's stead—the father who had never known of his existence. It was a strange chapter in human life—so strange that at first hardly anybody believed it; until, one by one, everybody got used to it, and accepted things as they were, without over-much questioning.

As, of course, all this change was likewise accepted at

the rectory. Mrs. Trevena looked a trifle paler—she had become excessively pale and thin within the past year; "worn to a shadow," people said; but she answered, with a peaceful smile, all the questions and congratulations. Only she never spoke of Sir Arthur except as "my son."

There was another thing which she had to settle; and be also congratulated upon, and that was "my son's marriage."

"You couldn't expect me to live in that big house all alone, mother," pleaded Arthur—with amusing simplicity. "And since I cannot possibly get you, why not let me have Nanny to take care of me?"

It did indeed seem the wisest plan. Though they were both so young—only nineteen and twenty-one—still they were not "foolish;" for both had already battled with the world sufficiently to gain premature wisdom. And perhaps after all, though this generation does not think so, early marriages, when not rash or improvident, are best. Our grandfathers and grandmothers, who did not wait to be rich, but began life simply, as their parents did before them, and spent together their fresh, unstained, hopeful youth, their busy maturity, their peaceful old age, were probably happier than we of today; who fritter away in idle flirting, or more harmful things, our blossoming time; marrying late in life with all the heart gone out of us; or never marrying at all, and then arguing sagely that to "fall in love" is a folly, and to marry is little less than a crime.

Mrs. Trevena did not think so—would not have thought so, even had her son been still "poor" Arthur
P

Trevena. When, now he was Sir Arthur Damerel, he began to speak of his marriage, all she suggested was that he should wait a year, out of respect to the dead; and to gain a little experience in managing his large property, for the good of the living.

"A year is a long time," said he disconsolately.

"Is it?" answered his mother, with a strange, far-away look, which startled him a moment, till he saw it melt into her usual smile. "Then let it be six months, my dear. Leave me Nanny, and stay you beside me for just six months more. Then—do as you will."

For the young people, neither of whom had seen the world, were determined, as soon as ever they were married, to go abroad and enjoy themselves; visiting Switzerland, Italy—perhaps even going on to Constantinople! They were so happy—so full of plans—so resolved to do no end of good on their estate; but they wanted just this little bit of pleasure—a harmless frolic together before they settled down.

And so the winter passed, very happily; Arthur being at the rectory almost as much as when he used to live there; but never failing to go back of nights to his large dull house. He also spent conscientiously every forenoon in his study with his steward, repairing much evil that had come about in his father's days, and planning no end of good to be done in his own. A happy time! full of hope for everybody. Nobody noticed much that Mrs. Trevena was the only one who smiled more than she spoke, and made no personal plans for the future at all.

She had had, ever since Sir Charles's funeral in the

chilly church, her usual winter cold; rather worse than usual; for she ceased to fight against it; left everything to Nanny and gradually kept entirely to the house, then to her own room—a new thing, which her husband could not understand at all. He went wandering about the rectory like a spirit in pain; or walked out into the village and wandered there, paying necessary or unnecessary pastoral visits, and telling everybody " that Mrs. Trevena had a bad cold, but would certainly be about again in a day or two." And sometimes, strong in this expectation, when he returned he would come to the foot of the stairs and call "Susannah!" just as usual; expecting her to come, as she always used to come, nobody knew from where—till he bethought himself to go in search of her to her room. There he always found her, and sat down content by her side.

But, beyond that room, always so cheerful and bright —with sunshine if there was any sun, with firelight if there was none, the house and he had to endure her absence, to learn to do without her. Under Nanny's charge all went on as usual—" the old original clock-work way," Arthur called it, and hoped his wife would keep his big house as well as his mother had kept this little one. But day after day there was the empty chair at the head of the table, the empty sofa by the drawing-room fire, the work-box that nobody opened, the book that nobody read.

Did any of them understand? Did Susannah herself understand? Who can tell?

There comes to us all a time when we begin to say, silently of course, our *Nunc dimittis*. We are tired—

so tired! Perhaps we ought not to be, and many good people would reprove us for being so, but we are tired—

> "We have had all the joys that the world could bestow,
> We have lived, we have loved."

Or else, we have had no joys, and have long since given up the hope of any. Which was scarcely Susannah's case, and yet she was tired.

When they left her alone—though they never did it for long—she would lean her head back against her pillows, with the weary look of one who waits for bed-time. All about her was so busy and bustling. One day she had watched her husband, hale and hearty, march down the garden to inquire about the first brood of chickens, and a February lamb.

"It will soon be spring," she said to herself, and listened to what seemed like a thrush's note in the garden; soon drowned by Arthur's piano below stairs, where he sat playing, with his "little Nanny" beside him—the girl who was almost as good as a wife to him already; taking care of him, guiding him, and adoring him by turns. "How happy he is—that boy!" and a tear or two dropped from Susannah's eyes: human tears! "I should like to have seen his children—just one little baby, like himself—my little baby that I loved so. It would have been the old days over again; when I sat in the rocking-chair—he in his night-gown, sucking his thumb, with his eyes fixed on my face, and his two little feet in one of my hands. Wasn't he a pretty baby?"

The last sentence was said aloud, and in French, to Manette—now grown stout and middle-aged, but with her faithful Swiss heart still devoted to her mistress, creeping up on every excuse from her cooking to see if Madame wanted anything.

No; Susannah's wants were few—as they always had been. She was an invalid who gave no trouble to anybody. The coming Angel came so stealthily, so peacefully, that no one ever heard his step.

"Stop a minute, Manette," she said, after a few minutes' cheerful chat. "I wish you would bring the rocking-chair out of the nursery—I mean Miss Nanny's room—dear me, how stupid I am growing! I should like to have it here."

Manette brought it: and when the young people came up-stairs—which they did very soon, for they were not selfish lovers—Arthur greeted it with a shout of delight, and declared it made him feel "like a little baby" once more. All that evening he insisted on sitting down on the floor at his mother's feet; and let her play with his curls, or what remained of them, for he was a fashionable young man now, and had his hair cut like other "golden youths." He told Nanny ridiculous stories of his childhood, making himself out to be twice as naughty as he ever had been; forcing even his mother to laugh, and laughing himself till the tears ran down his cheeks. In fact, cheerful and content as they always were at the rectory, they had seldom spent so merry an evening; the rector included—who came up from his Saturday night's sermon, put off as usual till the last minute—and begged to have tea in his wife's room.

"Everything seems so out of order down-stairs when you are not there, Susannah," said he restlessly. "You really must try to come down to-morrow. Now, pour out my tea, Nanny."

"No—not Nanny this time," her aunt said gently, and bidding Arthur move the table closer, she poured out her husband's tea, and gave it to him with her own hand—a rather shaky hand; as they remembered afterwards, and wondered they had never noticed it, nor how white and quiet she sat, long after the meal was over.

When Arthur had kissed his mother and bade her good-night, and Nanny came back, extra rosy, from the other rather lengthy good-night which always took place at the hall-door—she thought her aunt looked more tired than usual, and said so, offering to stay beside her for a while.

"Oh no!" Mrs. Trevena answered. "Let everybody go to bed, except Manette. She can sit with me till your uncle comes out of his study. Nanny,"—holding the girl's hand, and looking hard into her face—"you'll take care of your uncle? And—no, I need not tell you to take care of Arthur. Kiss me, my dear. Good-night."

That was all.

An hour later, Nanny was startled out of her happy sleep, as sound as a child's, to see Manette standing, white with terror, at her bedside. That had happened which nobody feared or expected—except, perhaps, the sufferer herself. A sudden and violent fit of coughing had produced hemorrhage of the lungs, and Mrs. Trevena was dying.

Nanny sprang out of her bed—she had had long experience in sick-nursing, enough to know that this was a question not of days or hours, but of minutes—that there was no time to summon anybody, that what help could be given must be given at once, by herself and Manette alone, for there was nobody to aid them, and no time to call anybody.

Susannah let them do all they could. She was quite conscious—smiled her thanks several times, but she never attempted to speak a word. Except once, when she heard Manette proposing to fetch Mr. Trevena, and motioned a feeble but decided negative.

"No, no! Save him from—from anything painful. Don't let him see me—till afterwards."

And so it befell that the breast upon which the parting soul relied was, not her husband's, not Arthur's, both so tenderly beloved, but Nanny's, whom she had always been kind to, and liked much without actually loving—Nanny, the blameless daughter of her lifelong foe.

There, just before midnight, while the rector was still busy over his sermon, and Arthur at Tawton Abbas was sleeping the sleep of healthy, happy youth, Susannah gradually lost all memory even of them, all consciousness of the world about her, and passed peacefully away into the world unknown.

When the two who to her had been so infinitely dear came to look at her, there was, as she had wished, "nothing painful"—only a beautiful image of eternal rest. Did she love them still? Who knows? Let us pray that it may be so.

 .   .   .   .

None can mourn for ever: it is not right they should. But it was a whole year before Arthur recovered from the blow which, to him, had fallen like a thunderbolt out of a clear sky. The young seldom realize death unless it comes quite close to them. It had never entered his mind that his mother would die—until she died. He could not imagine existence without her. The shock was so great, and the change it wrought in him so piteous, that Nanny was for a time absolutely terrified. Both the young people seemed to grow suddenly old. They spoke of love and marriage no more, but devoted themselves like a real son and daughter to the desolate man who had lost even more than they.

The rector was very quiet from first to last. Whether he grieved or not, no one could tell; from the day of her funeral he rarely mentioned his wife's name. But he often went wandering mournfully about the house as if in search of her, and then went silently back to his books; taking very little interest in anything else. He seemed to have suddenly turned into an old man—quite patient and quite helpless. It was not without cause that Nanny always answered when questioned about the date of her marriage, "I couldn't leave him; she told me to take care of him." In truth, for a long time all that the forlorn three appeared to think of was to do exactly as she had said, or would have wished.

And they were doing it, they felt sure, when, as the primroses of the second spring began to blossom over her grave, Arthur took courage and again asked for Nanny. The birds were singing, the little lambs bleating, the chickens chirping—all her young "family," as Susannah used to call them—the creatures whom she had so liked to see happy about her.

"She would like us to be happy, I know," Arthur said, when he urged the question, and insisted to Nanny that Manette was quite able to take charge of the rector now, and that she herself would not be more than a few minutes' walk from her uncle. When Mr. Trevena was told all this he assented without hesitation to the marriage. It did not much matter to him who took care of him now. He might live many years yet—the bookworm's placid self-absorbed life; but the half of himself was missing for ever.

So, one bright spring day, Arthur led his bride past his mother's grave. His mother would not have grieved: she would have been glad—as is the instinct of all unselfish souls.

> "On that grave drop not a tear . . .
> Rather smile there, blessed one,
> Thinking of me in the sun;
> Or forget me, smiling on."

But she was not forgotten—she never could be. She had lived long enough to make her boy all that he was; to form his mind and character, heart and soul: to fit him for the aims and duties of life; high aims and serious duties; for Sir Arthur Damerel is not the sort of man to hide himself, or submit to be hidden, under a bushel. His position must inevitably bring him many a responsibility, many a trouble and care; but he will fight through all, with his wife beside him—little Nanny, who has given the neighborhood an entirely new and revised edition of the Lady Damerels of Tawton Abbas. Active, energetic, kindly, benevolent—she is so well-loved both by rich and poor that no one stops to consider whether or not she is beautiful. Nor does her husband. To him she is simply "little Nanny."

One of their duties—not always a pleasant one—is their yearly visit of a day or two to the Dowager Lady Damerel, who has turned very religious, and is made much of in a select circle who have taken the title of "Believers," one of their points of belief being that nobody can be saved, except themselves. Such a creed is the natural outcome of that pleasure-loving egoism which had characterized her earlier days. The greater the sinner, the greater the saint—if such sainthood is worth anything. She takes very little interest in her son or his belongings; except perhaps in one very handsome baby grand-daughter, who she declares is just like herself; but they are on terms of the utmost politeness. Only he never calls her anything but "Lady Damerel." He feels that his real mother—"*my* mother," as he always speaks of her, and scarcely a day passes that he does not speak of her—was she who sleeps in that quiet grave within sight of the dining-room window of the dear old rectory.

And Susannah, had she known this, and seen how her influence will descend though Arthur to his children's children, would have died content, feeling that those one-and-twenty years had not been thrown away—that she had not only made her own life and her husband's happy—but, as good Dr. Franklin once said, she had "saved a soul alive."

www.ingramcontent.com/pod-product-compliance
Lightning Source LLC
Chambersburg PA
CBHW021817230426
43669CB00008B/780